PRAXIS® CORE Math 5732

By: Preparing Teachers In America

This page is intentionally left blank.

This page is intentionally left blank.

Free Online Email Tutoring Services

All preparation guides purchased directly from Preparing Teachers In America includes a free three month email tutoring subscription. Any resale of preparation guides does not qualify for a free email tutoring subscription.

What is Email Tutoring?

Email Tutoring allows buyers to send questions to tutors via email. Buyers can send any questions regarding the exam processes, strategies, content questions, or practice questions.

Preparing Teachers In America reserves the right not to answer questions with or without reason(s).

How to use Email Tutoring?

Buyers need to send an email to info@preparingteachersinamerica.com requesting email tutoring services. Buyers may be required to confirm the email address used to purchase the preparation guide or additional information prior to using email tutoring. Once email tutoring subscription is confirmed, buyers will be provided an email address to send questions to. The three month period will start the day the subscription is confirmed.

Any misuse of email tutoring services will result in termination of service. Preparing Teachers In America reserves the right to terminate email tutoring subscription at anytime with or without notice.

Comments and Suggestions

All comments and suggestions for improvements of the study guide and email tutoring services need to be sent to info@preparingteachersinamerica.com.

This page is intentionally left blank.

Table of Content

This page is intentionally left blank.

About the Exam and Study Guide

What is PRAXIS Core Academic Skills for Educators: Mathematic (5732)?

The PRAXIS Core Academic Skills for Educators: Mathematic 5732 is an exam to test potential teachers' competencies in basic math skills necessary to pursue a teaching career. The exam is aligned with the Common Core State Standards for Mathematics, and the exam covers the following content areas:

- Content Category I: Numbers and Quality (~30% of the exam)
- Content Category II: Algebra and Functions (~30% of the exam)
- Content Category III: Geometry (~20% of the exam)
- Content Category IV: Statistics and Probability (~20% of the exam)

The computer delivered exam includes an on-screen calculator. The exam is timed at 85 minutes and consists of 56 questions; some questions may not count toward the score. Questions can appear in three formats, which include the following:

- Selected-response questions – select one answer choice
- Selected-response questions – select one or more answer choices
- Numeric entry questions

What topics are covered on the exam?

The following are topics covered on the exam:

- Ratios and Proportional Relationships, The Real Number System, and Quantities
- Seeing Structure In Expression and Reasoning With Equations and Inequalities
- Functions
- Congruence, Similarity, Right Triangles, and Circles
- Geometric Measurement and Dimension
- Modeling in Geometry
- Basic Statistics and Probability
- Interpreting Categorical and Quantitative Data
- Making Influence and Justifying Conclusion
- Using Probability to Make Decisions

What is included in this study guide book?

This guide includes two full length practice exams for the PRAXIS CORE Math 5732 along with detail explanations. The recommendation is to take the exams under exam conditions of 85 minutes and a quiet environment.

This page is intentionally left blank.

Practice Exam 1

This page is intentionally left blank.

Exam Answer Sheet Exam 1

Below is an optional answer sheet to use to document answers.

Question Number	Selected Answer	Question Number	Selected Answer
1		29	
2		30	
3		31	
4		32	
5		33	
6		34	
7		35	
8		36	
9		37	
10		38	
11		39	
12		40	
13		41	
14		42	
15		43	
16		44	
17		45	
18		46	
19		47	
20		48	
21		49	
22		50	
23		51	
24		52	
25		53	
26		54	
27		55	
28		56	

This page is intentionally left blank.

Full Math Practice Exam 1

QUESTION 1

Mark has a writing assignment due in 5 days. In order to complete it, he plans to write 15 pages during one day and writes 5 pages each remaining day as he proofreads. How many pages does Mark plan to write?

$15 + 4.5$

- A. 20
- B. 30
- C. 35
- D. 40
- E. 45

Answer:

QUESTION 2

Write the answer in the box below.   25   10

Juan budgets $\frac{1}{4}$ of his monthly salary for clothing, and two months ago he spent $\frac{1}{10}$ of his monthly salary on clothing. What fraction of his budget was spent on clothing two months ago?

Answer:

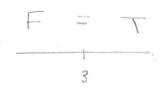

QUESTION 3

Circle all correct answers.

$$-3x + 15 < 6$$

$x > 3$

Which of the following values of x are solutions to the inequality above?

  -1.65   0.75   2.89   (3.21)   3.00   (3.14)

Answer:

QUESTION 4

Which of the following is equivalent to 6.25?

 A. 56/9

 B. 36/5

 C. 48/7

 (D.) 25/4

 E. 13/2

$$\frac{4 \cdot 6}{4} + \frac{1}{4}$$

$$\frac{24}{4} + \frac{1}{4}$$

$$\frac{625}{100} \qquad \frac{25}{4}$$

$$\frac{25}{}$$

Answer:

QUESTION 5

Kyle jogs at least 20 minutes, and then, he works out for an hour and ten minutes. What is the minimum amount of time in minutes he uses to complete his physical activities?

 A. 90 minutes

 B. 100 minutes

 C. 130 minutes

 D. 150 minutes

 E. 180 minutes

Answer:

QUESTION 6

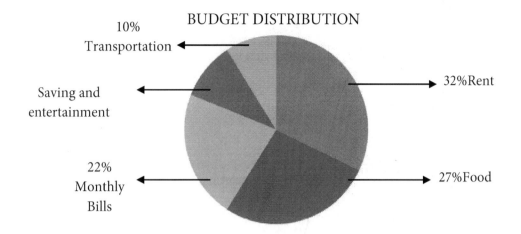

BUDGET DISTRIBUTION

10% Transportation

Saving and entertainment

32%Rent

22% Monthly Bills

27%Food

The graph above shows the percent of Mary's monthly budget distributed into her most important expenses. What percent of her monthly budget can she use for saving and entertainment?

    A. 8%

    B. 9%

    C. 10%

    D. 11%

    E. 12%

Answer:

QUESTION 7

Tom buys a package that contains 432 marbles. If he seeks to distribute packs of 15 marbles to his classmates, what is the total number of complete packs that he can make?

    A. 22

    B. 28

    C. 29

    D. 30

    E. 32

Answer:

$a + \textcircled{b} + 180^\circ$ $a + 3a = 180$

$b = \textcircled{3a}$ $a = 45$

QUESTION 8

Write the answer in the box below.

45

$a + \textcircled{b} = 180^\circ$

$a + \textcircled{3a} = 180^\circ$ $4a = 180^\circ$

$4a = 180$ $a = 45$

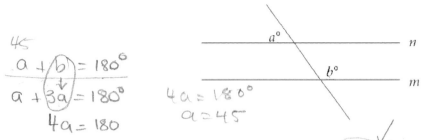

In the figure above, line n and line m are parallel, and b = 3a. What is the value of a?

$\dfrac{b-a}{3}$

$b = 3a$

45

Answer:

QUESTION 9

Which of the following units is the most reasonable in measuring the height of a person?

    A. mile

    B. kilometer

    C. kilogram

    D. centimeter

    E. millimeter

Answer:

QUESTION 10

Month	Miles Driven
January	2600
February	3000
March	3200
April	2400
May	1800
June	
July	3400
August	3200
September	2500
October	2700
November	1900
December	2200

The table above shows the approximate number of miles driven by Bill during each month in the past year. How many miles did Bill drive during June if the arithmetic mean of the miles driven for the entire year was 2600?

    A. 2300 miles

    B. 2400 miles

    C. 2500 miles

    D. 2550 miles

    E. 2600 miles

Answer:

QUESTION 11

What digit is located in the tens place for the number 4,654.702?

    A. 0

    B. 2

    C. 4

    D. 5

    E. 6

Answer:

QUESTION 12

In a map displaying the freeway system, 1 inch is represented by 200 miles. How many inches on the map represent a freeway of 2,460 miles of length?

    A. 9.6

    B. 9.8

    C. 10.8

    D. 12.3

    E. 12.8

Answer:

$$\frac{1}{200} = \frac{x}{2460}$$

$$2460 = 200x$$

$$\frac{2460}{200} =$$

QUESTION 13

For the calculation of $134,126 \div 1,987$, which of the following is the closest approximation?

    A. 48

    B. 67

    C. 72

    D. 97

    E. 130

Answer:

$$\frac{130,000}{2000}$$

QUESTION 14

Write the answer in the box below.

If 25 is p percent of 50, what is p percent of 80?

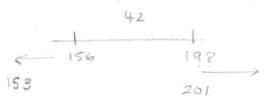

[box]

Answer:

QUESTION 15

156, 176, 198, x, 165

The range calculated for the above data is 45. Determine the missing value, x?

    A. 111
    B. 153
    C. 178
    D. 200
    E. 225

42

156   198

153   201

Answer:

QUESTION 16

Write the answer in the box below.

$$\sqrt{(8 \times 72)} =$$

8.3

24

Answer:

-3 . 4

3 √37 √x/ 4

QUESTION 17

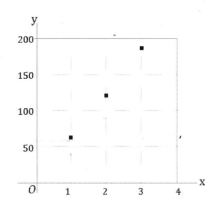

What relationship can be represented by the data points in the graph above?

A. hours and minutes
B. meters and inches
C. meters and yards
D. weeks and months
E. days and weeks

Answer:

QUESTION 18

If x-2y=0 and -2x+y=2, then 3x-3y=

    A. -4

    B. -2

    C. 0

    D. 3

    E. 4

Answer:

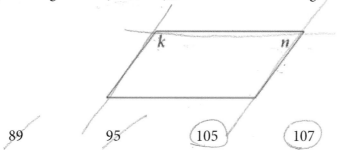

$$x - 2y = 0$$
$$+2x \mp y = 2$$
$$\overline{}$$
$$3x - 3y = -2$$

$$x - 2y = 0$$
$$-(-2x + y) = -2$$

QUESTION 19

Circle <u>all</u> such answers.

The figure is a parallelogram. If 65 < k < 80, select all the following that could be the value of n?

$$\boxed{K + n = 180}$$
$$65$$
$$89$$

    89   95   (105)   (107)   118

Answer:

                                  100   115

                                  K

QUESTION 20

Card Collection Data

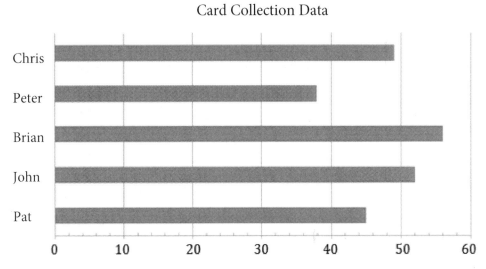

Five kids meet to play a trading card game. The number of cards each kid had initially is shown in the graph above. After the game, Pat had 28; John had 45; Brian had 52; and Chris had 63. How many cards does Peter have after the game?

52   50   49

    A. 10

    37 or 38

    B. 28

    C. 38

    D. 52

    E. 56

Answer:

16

QUESTION 21

The following formula gives the volume of a sphere:

$$\text{Volume of Sphere} = \frac{4}{3} \times \pi \times r^3$$

What is the volume in cubic inches of spherical balloon that has a diameter of 8 inches?

   A. $\frac{256}{3}\pi$

   B. $\frac{512}{3}\pi$

   C. $\frac{64}{3}\pi$

   D. $\frac{2048}{3}\pi$

   E. $\frac{128}{3}\pi$

$$\frac{4 \quad 4 \cdot 4 \cdot 4}{3} \pi$$

Answer:

QUESTION 22

Brand A sells erasers in packages of 4, while Brand B sells erasers in packages of 3. If Donna buys 12 packages of Brand A, then how many packages of Brand B does she have to buy to get the same quantity?

   A. 18

   B. 16

   C. 14

   D. 12

   E. 10

Answer:

QUESTION 23

Which of the following numbers has a square that is less than itself?

   A. -3   9

   B. 0   0

   C. 0.3   .09

   D. 3

   E. 3.2

Answer:

QUESTION 24

0.376544376544376544376544…

In the decimal number above, the first six digits to the right of the decimal point repeat indefinitely in the same order. What is the 326th digit to the right of the decimal point?

A. 3
B. 4
C. 5
D. 6
E. 7

Answer:

QUESTION 25

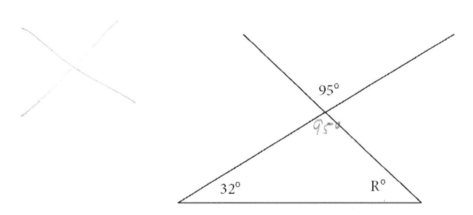

From the figure above, determine the value of the angle, R.

A. 32°
B. 37°
C. 39°
D. 53°
E. 58°

Answer:

QUESTION 26

In a classroom, 19 kids have at least one brother and 13 kids have at least one sister. Of the kids who have a brother or a sister, 8 have both a brother and a sister. If there are 35 kids in the class, how many kids do NOT have any siblings?

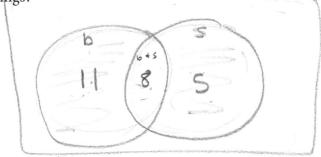

    A. 15
    B. 12
    C. 14
    D. 11
    E. 9

Answer:

QUESTION 27

If x is divisible by 8, then it is divisible by 6

The above statement is false, if x equals:

    A. 6
    B. 14
    C. 48
    D. 64
    E. 96

Answer:

QUESTION 28

Use the chart below for the next three questions.

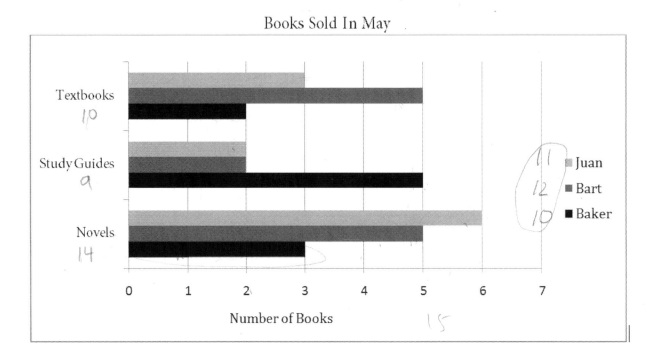

Books Sold In May

Which type of book was sold the most?
  A. Textbooks
  B. Study Guides
  C. Novels
  D. Textbooks and Novels
  E. All were equally sold

Answer:

QUESTION 29

The above chart shows the different types of books sold by Juan, Bart, and Baker in the month of May. What is the mean of the books sold by the three individuals?

    A. 10
    B. 11
    C. 12
    D. 13
    E. 14

Answer:

QUESTION 30

Of the three types of books, which of the three books contains the value of the mode?

    I.   Textbooks
    II.   Study Guides
    III.   Novels

A. II only
B. I and II
C. I and III
D. I, II, and III
E. II and II

Answer:

3, 5, 2, 2, 2.5, 6, 5, 3.

2 modes   "2 books"
          "5 books"

QUESTION 31

Bill is ten years older than his sister. If Bill was twenty-five years of age in 1983, in what year could he have been born?

    A. 1948
    B. 1953
    C. 1958
    D. 1963
    E. 1968

Answer:

QUESTION 32

The following are the scores Todd made on his exams during the Spring Semester: 90, 90, 90, 77, 75, 100, 84, 82 and 71. The instructor drops the two lowest scores and replaces those scores with the two highest scores. What is the average of Todd's scores?

    A. 84.33
    B. 89.22
    C. 99.22
    D. 90.00
    E. 90.33

Answer:

77 82 84 90 90 90 90 100 100
83 92 94   90   90   110

720
83

QUESTION 33

John had two grocery bags, and they were weighed to the nearest kilogram. The bags weighed 33kg and 43kg. If the combined weight was W kg, which is true?

    A. $76.5 \leq W \leq 77$

    B. $72 \leq W \leq 73$

    C. $74.5 \leq W \leq 75.5$

    D. $75.5 \leq W \leq 76.5$

    E. $76.5 \leq W \leq 77.5$

Answer:

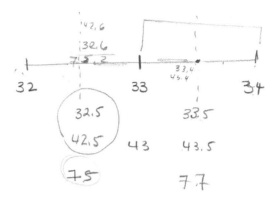

QUESTION 34

The width of Marty's backyard is 43.2 feet and the length is 32.1 feet. What is the area of the rectangular shaped backyard?

    A. 150.5 feet²

    B. 160.6 feet²

    C. 150.6 feet²

    D. 1386.72 feet²

    E. 1368.72 feet²

Answer:

$$A = \ell \cdot w$$

23

QUESTION 35

Circle all such answers.

Of the following, which is/are greater than 1.25?

125%	3/2	150%	2/3	12.5%

(handwritten annotations:) 125% → 1.25, 3/2 → 1.5 (circled) ✓, 150% → 1.50 (circled) ✓, 2/3 → .66, 12.5% → .125

Answer:

QUESTION 36

If x is a real number and integer and completes the solution $x^4 = 16$, which statement is true?

A. x is less than 4 ✓
B. x is greater than 4
C. x is less than 2 ✓
D. x = 2 *(circled)*
E. x = 4

(handwritten annotations:) x = -2 or +2; 4·4·4·4; 2·2·2·2; x = -2; $x^2 = 4$; +3 -3; $x^4 = 64$; x = 4, x = -4

Answer:

QUESTION 37

Sports Day Teams

Number of Teams	Students Per Team
4	3
2	8
6	2

(handwritten annotations:) 12, 16, 12, total 40

From the chart, how many total students are there?

A. 12
B. 13
C. 40 *(circled)*
D. 44
E. 23

Answer:

24

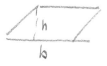

QUESTION 38

If the area of a triangle is $A = \frac{1}{2} \times b \times h$, then what would be the area of two triangles of the same size and shape?

A. $2 \times h$
B. $b \times h$ ⟨circled⟩
C. $2 \times b \times h$
D. $b^2 h^2$
E. A and B

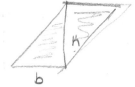

Answer:

$$A = \frac{1}{2} b h$$

$$\frac{1}{2} bh + \frac{1}{2} bh = bh$$

QUESTION 39

The following expressions are given:

$$Q = 4x - 3x + 18 \quad = 19$$
$$W = 2x + 4x \quad = 6$$
$$A = 4x + 2x + 1 \quad = 7$$
$$B = \frac{3x + 2x + 19}{12} \quad = \frac{24}{12} = 2$$

Which of the following provides the largest value if the value of x is 1?

A. Q ⟨circled⟩
B. W
C. A
D. B
E. A and B

Answer:

QUESTION 40

Circle all such answers.

If Q is a negative integer, select all that must result in a positive integer?

-10

$\overbrace{-(Q)-1}$ $\boxed{Q^2}$ $\cancel{Q+1}$

Answer:

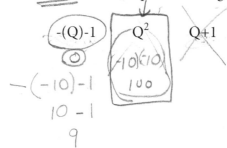

$-(-10)-1$

$10-1$

9

QUESTION 41

A circular pool is 300 yards in circumference. What is the radius of the pool?

  A. $130/\pi$
  B. $\boxed{150/\pi}$
  C. $175/\pi$
  D. $190/\pi$
  E. $300/\pi$

Answer:

$A = \pi r^2$

$C = \pi \cdot d = 2\pi r$

$\dfrac{300}{2\pi} = \dfrac{2\pi r}{2\pi}$

QUESTION 42

How many square feet of carpeting are needed to cover the area pictured below?

$4 = 2 \cdot 2$,

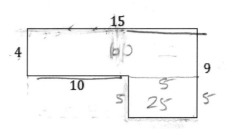

15

4

9

10

5

5

25

5

A. 45 square feet
B. 55 square feet
C. 65 square feet
D. 85 square feet
E. 87 square feet

135 –
– 50

Answer:

QUESTION 43

$\dfrac{r \cdot t}{t} = \dfrac{d}{t}$

$r = \dfrac{d}{t}$

Write the answer in the box below.

James walked 3 feet and 3 inches. The walk took 16 minutes and 15 seconds. What speed was James walking at?

36 in

| 0.04 | in/second |

$\dfrac{39 \text{ in}}{975 \text{ sec}}$

Answer:

QUESTION 44

The table below shows the number of students who passed the math test with an "A" during a 5 month period:

Month	Number of Students
January	4
February	2
March	4
April	3
May	3

What is/are all the mode(s) from the data provided?

    A. 2

    B. 3

    C. 4

    D. 3 and 4

    E. 2 and 3

Answer:

QUESTION 45

If 3.49212×10^5 is expanded to an ordinary number, what number will be in the hundreds place?

   A. 4
   B. 9
   C. 2
   D. 3
   E. 1

Answer:

QUESTION 46

What is $50\frac{1}{2}\%$ expressed as a fraction in lowest terms?

   A. 101/2
   B. 100/2
   C. 51/100
   D. 50/2
   E. 2/1

Answer:

QUESTION 47

In John's house, there are rooms for Joey and Victor. The length of Victor's room is 18 feet, and the length of Joey's room is twice as large. The width of Victor's room is 12 feet. What is the area of both rooms combined together?

   A. Cannot be solved.
   B. 216
   C. 432
   D. 423
   E. 261

Answer:

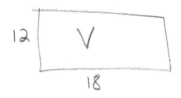

QUESTION 48

If both a rectangle and a circle lie on a plane, determine the maximum number of intersection points?

   A. 2
   B. 3
   C. 4
   D. 6
   E. 8

Answer:

QUESTION 49

A distributor of clothing has three different types of packages. The first package can fit 10 shirts; the second package can fit 12 shirts; and the third package can fit 16 shirts. Large boxes using only one type of package will be made. If these boxes are required to have the same number of shirts, what is the smallest possible total number of shirts in one box?

   A. 180
   B. 220
   C. 240
   D. 260
   E. 280

Answer:

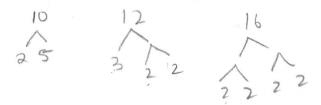

10   20   30   40   50   60

12   24   48

16   32   64

10   12   16

2 5   3   2 2   2 2 2 2

2,5 · 3, 2, 2, 2

240

30

QUESTION 50

Write the answer in the box below.

8"

If the perimeter of the rectangle above is 64 inches, what is the width?

Answer:

QUESTION 51

Write the answer in the box below.

Six people plan to buy a computer for their coworker, sharing the cost equally. If one person decided not to participate, the cost per person for the other five people would go up by $16. What is the cost of the present?

480

3 16
    5
(8 0)
    6

Answer:

QUESTION 52

Write the answer in the box below.

At an office, the manager earns 40% more than a first year employee. The employee earns what fraction of the manager's earnings?

Answer:

QUESTION 53

Write the answer in the box below.

If, $2.5 (z - 8) = 4.5z - 18$, then $z + 2 =$

Answer:

QUESTION 54

Write the answer in the box below.

One pen costs \$0.30 and one marker costs \$0.25. At those prices, what is the total cost of 18 pens and 100 markers?

Answer:

QUESTION 55

Which of the following units is best for measuring the distance from Houston to Chicago?

    A. millimeter
    B. kilometer
    C. meter
    D. centigram
    E. milligram

Answer:

QUESTION 56

Circle <u>all</u> such answers.

What are the positive integer factors of 12?

          1   2   3   4   6   8   12

Answer:

This page is intentionally left blank.

Answer Key and Content Category Exam 1

Question Number	Correct Answer	Content Category	Question Number	Correct Answer	Content Category
1	C	II	29	B	IV
2	2/5	II	30	D	IV
3	3.21,3.14	II	31	C	I
4	D	I	32	B	IV
5	A	II	33	D	I
6	B	IV	34	D	III
7	B	I	35	3/2,150%	I
8	45°	III	36	D	I
9	D	III	37	C	I
10	A	IV	38	B	III
11	D	I	39	A	I
12	D	II	40	Q^2	I
13	B	I	41	B	III
14	40	I	42	D	III
15	B	IV	43	0.4	II
16	24	I	44	D	IV
17	A	IV	45	C	I
18	B	II	46	A	I
19	105,107	III	47	A	II
20	D	IV	48	E	III
21	A	III	49	C	II
22	B	II	50	24	III
23	C	I	51	$480	II
24	E	I	52	5/7	II
25	D	III	53	1	II
26	D	II	54	$30.40	II
27	D	I	55	B	II
28	C	IV	56	1,2,3,4,6,12	I

NOTE: Getting approximately 80% of the questions correct increases chances of obtaining passing score on the real exam. This varies from different states and university programs.

This page is intentionally left blank.

Full Math Practice Questions Explanations Exam 1

QUESTION 1

Mark has a writing assignment due in 5 days. In order to complete the assignment, he plans to write 15 pages during one day and writes 5 pages each remaining day as he proofreads. How many pages does Mark plan to write?

   A. 20
   B. 30
   C. 35
   D. 40
   E. 45

Answer: C

Explanation: Mark plans to write for a total of 5 days. On the first day he writes 15 pages, and on the following four days, he writes 5 pages each day. Two methods can be used to solve for the total number of pages he plans to write:

Method 1: Knowing that he will write 5 pages for 4 days, multiply 5 by 4, and add 15 (from the first day) to get the total value.

$$15+(4\times5) = 35 \text{ pages}$$

Method 2: Simply add the following to obtain the answer:

$$15+5+5+5+5 = 35 \text{ pages}$$

QUESTION 2

Write the answer in the box below.

Juan budgets $\frac{1}{4}$ of his monthly salary for clothing, and two months ago he spent $\frac{1}{10}$ of his monthly salary on clothing. What fraction of his budget was spent on clothing two months ago?

Answer: $\frac{2}{5}$

Explanation: The total monthly salary for clothing is $\frac{2}{5}$. Two months ago he only spent $\frac{1}{10}$. To obtain the fraction of Juan's budget spent on clothing two months ago, divide the fraction:

$$\frac{\text{fraction } \textbf{spent} \text{ two months ago}}{\text{fraction of monthly budgeted amount}} = \frac{\frac{1}{10}}{\frac{1}{4}} = \frac{1}{10} \times \frac{4}{1} = \frac{4}{10} \div \frac{2}{2} = \frac{2}{5}$$

QUESTION 3

Circle all correct answers.

$$-3x + 15 < 6$$

Which of the following values of x are solutions to the inequality above?

| -1.65 | 0.75 | 2.89 | 3.21 | 3.00 | 3.14 |

Answer: 3.21 and 3.14

Explanation: The following steps are to solve the inequality:

Step 1: Subtract 15 both sides

$$-3x + 15 - 15 < 6 - 15$$
$$-3x < -9$$

Step 2: Divide both sides by -3. Multiplying and dividing inequalities by negative number requires flipping the inequality sign.

$$\frac{-3x}{-3} < \frac{-9}{-3}$$
$$x > 3$$

All choices greater than 3 are the answers, which are 3.21 and 3.14.

QUESTION 4

Which of the following is equivalent to 6.25?

    A. 56/9

    B. 36/5

    C. 48/7

    D. 25/4

    E. 13/2

Answer: D

Explanation: There are two methods to complete this problem.

Method 1: Given a decimal number and given answer choices as fractions, convert the decimal to a fraction. The first step would be to move two units to the right to obtain a whole number, which gives:

$$625$$

Then, divide the number by 100 and reduce the fraction. To reduce the fraction, divide the top and bottom by 25.

$$\frac{625}{100} \div \frac{25}{25} = \frac{25}{4}$$

Method 2: This method is the preferred approach for this problem. Recognize that 0.25 is equal to $\frac{1}{4}$. With this knowledge, convert the decimal to a mixed fraction:

$$6\frac{1}{4}$$

Then, convert the mixed number into an improper fraction as the answer choices are in improper fraction form, which the gives final answer:

$$\frac{25}{4}$$

QUESTION 5

Kyle jogs at least 20 minutes, and then he works out for an hour and ten minutes. What is the minimum amount of time in minutes he uses to complete his physical activities?

A. 90 minutes
B. 100 minutes
C. 130 minutes
D. 150 minutes
E. 180 minutes

Answer: A

Explanation: Add the minutes for Kyle's physical activities. Kyle jogs for 20 minutes and works out for an hour and ten minutes, which is equivalent to 70 minutes. Adding 20 minutes and 70 minutes gives a total of 90 minutes.

QUESTION 6

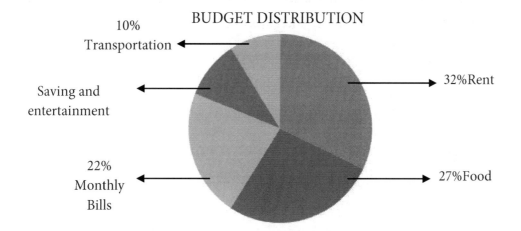

The graph above shows the percent of Mary's monthly budget distributed into her most important expenses. What percent of her monthly budget can she use for saving and entertainment?

    A. 8%

    B. 9%

    C. 10%

    D. 11%

    E. 12%

Answer: B

Explanation: The question is asking to figure out the monthly budget Mary uses for saving and entertainment. From the chart, add up all the percents and subtract the result from 100 %

$$10\%+22\%+32\%+27\% = 91\%$$
$$100\ \%-91\ \% = 9\ \%$$

QUESTION 7

Tom buys a package that contains 432 marbles. If he seeks to distribute packs of 15 marbles to his classmates, what is the total number of complete packs that he can make?

    A. 22

    B. 28

    C. 29

    D. 30

    E. 32

Answer: B

Explanation: In order to determine the number of complete packs Tom can make, divide the total number of marbles (432) by the number marbles he wants in each pack (15). For this problem, the interest is in the whole number as the question is asking for the complete number of packages.

$$432 \div 15 = 28.8$$

Therefore, the final answer is 28 packs.

QUESTION 8

Write the answer in the box below.

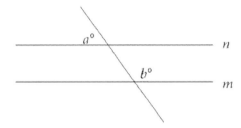

In the figure above, line n and line m are parallel, and b = 3a. What is the value of a?

Answer: 45°

Explanation: The sum of the measures of supplementary angle is 180°. That is a+b = 180. The question states that b=3a. Substituting for b results in 4a=180, giving a=45°.

QUESTION 9

Which of the following units is the most reasonable in measuring the height of a person?

    A. mile

    B. kilometer

    C. kilogram

    D. centimeter

    E. millimeter

Answer: D

Explanation: The most reasonable choice would be D. Answer choice A and B are used to determine long distances while answer choice E are used to determine short lengths. Answer choice C is used for weighing purposes, which has nothing to do with measuring length.

QUESTION 10

Month	Miles Driven
January	2600
February	3000
March	3200
April	2400
May	1800
June	
July	3400
August	3200
September	2500
October	2700
November	1900
December	2200

The table above shows the approximate number of miles driven by Bill during each month in the past year. How many miles did Bill drive during June if the arithmetic mean of the miles driven for the entire year was 2600?

    A. 2300 miles

    B. 2400 miles

    C. 2500 miles

    D. 2550 miles

    E. 2600 miles

Answer: A

Explanation: The mean value is given, so multiply the mean (2600) by the number of months in the table, which is 12.

$$2,600 \times 12 = 31,200 \text{ miles}$$

The total number of miles driven must equal 31,200. To determine the missing value for June, add up all the miles provided in the table, which will be 28,900 miles (use a calculator to compute). The last step would be to subtract 28,900 from 31,200 to obtain the final answer of 2,300 miles (use calculator to compute).

QUESTION 11

What digit is located in the tens place for the number 4,654.702?

    A. 0

    B. 2

    C. 4

    D. 5

    E. 6

Answer: D

Explanation: Based on the place value system, the number 5 is in the tens place.

QUESTION 12

In a map displaying the freeway system, 1 inch is represented by 200 miles. How many inches on the map represent a freeway of 2,460 miles of length?

    A. 9.6

    B. 9.8

    C. 10.8

    D. 12.3

    E. 12.8

Answer: D

Explanation: This is a proportion problem requiring cross multiplication to solve for the missing value. NOTE: Use a calculator for computation.

$$\frac{1 \text{ inch}}{200 \text{ miles}} = \frac{x \text{ inches}}{2,460 \text{ miles}}$$

After cross multiplying:

$$2,460 = 200 \times x$$

Divide both sides by 200, giving the final answer:

$$\frac{2,460}{200} = \frac{200 \times x}{200}$$

$$x = 12.3 \text{ inches}$$

QUESTION 13

For the calculation of 134,126÷1,987, which of the following is the closest approximation?

    A. 48

    B. 67

    C. 72

    D. 97

    E. 130

Answer: B

Explanation: For this problem, estimate the given values. The value of 134,126 should be rounded to 134,000, and the value of 1,987 should be rounded to 2,000. After that, perform the division operation to obtain the final answer.

$$134,000 \div 2,000 = 67$$

Note: Calculator can be used for computation.

QUESTION 14

Write the answer in the box below.

If 25 is p percent of 50, what is p percent of 80?

Answer: 40

Explanation: Use the information in the question to write out equations.

- "If 25 is p percent of 50" is the same as "25 = p% x 50" in equation form.
- "what is p percent of 80" is the same as y = p% x 80 in equation form.

Keywords to remember for the exam:

- "what is" means a variable (unknown)
- "is" means equal sign
- "of" means multiply

The question is asking to find the value of y. To do that, solve for "p%" in equation "25 = p% x 50" by dividing both sides by 50, which gives p%=0.5. Insert the value of p% into equation "y = p% x 80" to get y = 0.5 x 80 = 40.

QUESTION 15

156, 176, 198, x, 165

The range calculated for the above data is 45. Determine the missing value, x?

    A. 111

    B. 153

    C. 178

    D. 200

    E. 225

Answer: B

Explanation: The range between the highest and the lowest known values is 198 − 156 = 42. Therefore, the highest value has to be increased by 3 or the lowest value decreased by 3. The numbers become 201 and 153. Answer option B is 153, which is the answer.

QUESTION 16

Write the answer in the box below.

$$\sqrt{(8\times72)} =$$

Answer: 24

Explanation: Use a calculator to solve the problem. Insert 8×72 (gives 576) in the calculator and then click the square root button. The answer is 24.

QUESTION 17

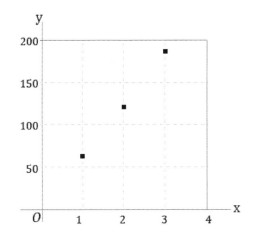

What relationship can be represented by the data points in the graph above?

    A. hours and minutes

    B. meters and inches

    C. meters and yards

    D. weeks and months

    E. days and weeks

Answer: A

Explanation: Look at the data points (1, 60), (2, 120), and (3, 180). The relationship shown is for hours and minutes. 1 hour = 60 minutes, 2 hours = 120 minutes, and 3 hours = 180 minutes.

QUESTION 18

If x-2y=0 and -2x+y=2, then 3x-3y=

    A. -4

    B. -2

    C. 0

    D. 3

    E. 4

Answer: B

Explanation: To find the value of 3x-3y, subtract the equations given. Remember to distribute the negative sign, which will change all the signs in the second equation.

$$x-2y = 0$$
$$\underline{-1(-2x+y)= -1(2)}$$
$$= 3x - 3y = -2$$

NOTE: The answer to this problem can be reached by solving for x and y, which is a longer process. Doing long calculations and processes during the exam might be indication there is a hidden trick to solve the problem.

QUESTION 19

Circle <u>all</u> such answers.

The figure is a parallelogram. If $65 < k < 80$, select all the following that could be the value of n?

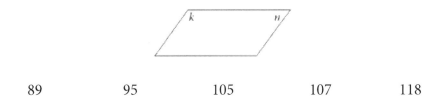

89   95   105   107   118

Answer: 105 and 107

Explanation: The problem gives a range for k. Using the lower limit of the range, 65, the value of n can be found by: $180 - 65 = 115$. Using the upper limit of the range, 80, the value of n can be found by: $180 - 80 = 100$. The answer has to be between 100 and 115. The answers are 105 and 107.

QUESTION 20

Card Collection Data

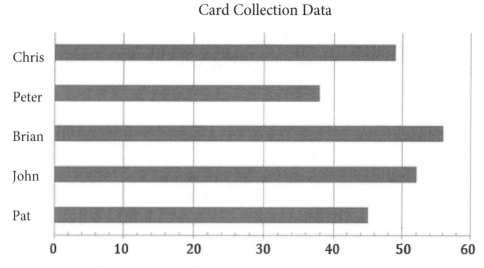

Five kids meet to play a trading card game. The number of cards each kid had initially is shown in the graph above. After the game, Pat had 28; John had 45; Brian had 52; and Chris had 63. How many cards does Peter have after the game?

    A. 10
    B. 28
    C. 38
    D. 52
    E. 56

Answer: D

Explanation: The question asks to find the number of cards Peter has after the game. Add all number of cards from the chart ($45 + 52 + 56 + 38 + 49 = 240$). The total is 240. Then, subtract the amount of cards the other people have after the game.

$$240 - 28 - 45 - 52 - 63 = 52$$

QUESTION 21

The following formula give the volume of a sphere:

$$\text{Volume of Sphere} = \frac{4}{3} \times \pi \times r^3$$

What is the volume in cubic inches of spherical balloon that has a diameter of 8 inches?

    A. $\frac{256}{3}\pi$

    B. $\frac{512}{3}\pi$

    C. $\frac{64}{3}\pi$

    D. $\frac{2048}{3}\pi$

    E. $\frac{128}{3}\pi$

Answer: A

Explanation:

The following formula is the volume of a sphere:

$$\text{Volume of Sphere} = \frac{4}{3} \times \pi \times r^3$$

Knowing the diameter gives the value of the radius, which is 4. The answer choices are in terms of π, so leave that in the answer without performing the numerical multiplication.

$$\text{Volume of Sphere} = \frac{4}{3} \times \pi \times 4^3$$
$$\text{Volume of Sphere} = \frac{4}{3} \times \pi \times 64$$
$$\text{Volume of Sphere} = \frac{256}{3} \times \pi$$

QUESTION 22

Brand A sells erasers in packages of 4, while Brand B sells erasers in packages of 3. If Donna buys 12 packages of Brand A, then how many packages of Brand B does she have to buy to get the same quantity?

    A. 18
    B. 16
    C. 14
    D. 12
    E. 10

Answer: B

Explanation: Donna brought 12 packages of Brand A, which contained 4 erasers, so multiply 12 and 4, which gives her a total of 48 erasers. Brand B contains 3 erasers. To obtain the number of Brand B packages she needs to buy to obtain 48 erasers, divide 48 by 3, which gives 16 packages.

QUESTION 23

Which of the following numbers has a square that is less than itself?

    A. -3
    B. 0
    C. 0.3
    D. 3
    E. 3.2

Answer: C

Explanation: Numbers less than 1 and greater than 0 provide a square that is less than itself. Square of 0 is 0. Square of numbers larger than 1 provide a square that is larger than itself. Numbers given by $0<x<1$ are the only numbers that have squares less than themselves.

QUESTION 24

$$0.37654437654437654437654437654 4\ldots$$

In the decimal number above, the first six digits to the right of the decimal point repeat indefinitely in the same order. What is the 326th digit to the right of the decimal point?

    A. 3

    B. 4

    C. 5

    D. 6

    E. 7

Answer: E

Explanation: The first six digits are of a pattern that continues. To determine the 326th digit, divide 326 by 6, which gives 54 with remainder of 2. With the remainder being 2, go to the second number of the pattern to obtain the answer, which is 7.

QUESTION 25

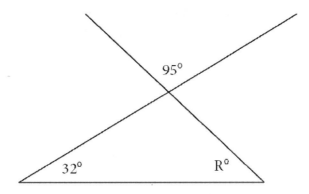

From the figure above, determine the value of the angle, R.

    A. 32°

    B. 37°

    C. 39°

    D. 53°

    E. 58°

Answer: D

Explanation: The sum of angles of a triangle is 180°. One of the angle values is directly given as 32°. The other value can be obtained from the information of 95° as the opposite angle would be the same. All values of the angle for the triangle are known except for one, which can be solved by:

$$180° - 95° - 32° = 53°$$

QUESTION 26

In a classroom, 19 kids have at least one brother and 13 kids have at least one sister. Of the kids who have a brother or a sister, 8 have both a brother and a sister. If there are 35 kids in the class, how many kids do NOT have any siblings?

    A. 15

    B. 12

    C. 14

    D. 11

    E. 9

Answer: D

Explanation: To determine the number of kids that do not have siblings, determine the total number of kids that do have brothers and sisters. From the problem, 19 kids have brothers and 13 kids have sisters, so total number of kids that have brothers and sisters is 32. However, 8 kids have both brothers and sisters, so subtract 8 from 32 to prevent double counting of those who have both brothers and sisters. The total number of kids that have a brother or a sister is 24 kids. To determine the number of kids that do not have siblings, subtract 24 from the total number of kids in class (35 kids), which gives the final answer of 11 kids.

QUESTION 27

If x is divisible by 8, then it is divisible by 6

The above statement is false, if x equals:

    A. 6

    B. 14

    C. 48

    D. 64

    E. 96

Answer: D

Explanation: First, eliminate all the answer choices that are not divisible by 8, which eliminates A and B. To make the statement false, find an answer choice that is not divisible by 6, which is D.

QUESTION 28

Use the chart below for the next three questions.

Books Sold In May

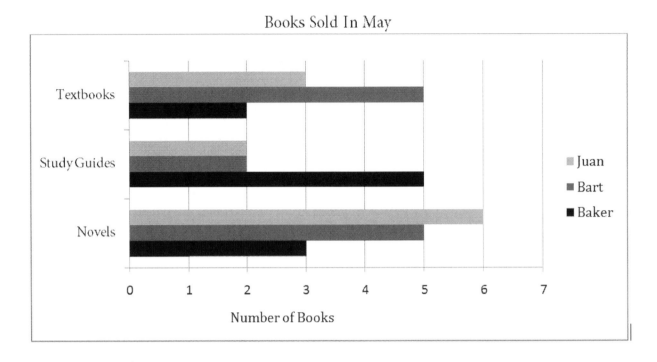

Which type of book was sold the most?
- A. Textbooks
- B. Study Guides
- C. Novels
- D. Textbooks and Novels
- E. All were equally sold

Answer: C

Explanation: When calculating the total number of each type of book that was sold, novels had the highest number at 14. Textbooks ranked second with 10 sold, while study guides ranked last with only 9 sold.

QUESTION 29

The above chart shows the different types of books sold by Juan, Bart, and Baker in the month of May. What is the mean of the books sold by the three individuals?

    A. 10

    B. 11

    C. 12

    D. 13

    E. 14

Answer: B

Explanation: To determine the mean value, add all the number of books sold.

$$3+5+2+2+5+5+6+5+3=33$$

Divide 33 by 3 as there are three individuals, giving the answer of 11.

QUESTION 30

Of the three types of books, which of the three books contains the value of the mode?

    I.   Textbooks

    II.   Study Guides

    III.   Novels

    A. II only

    B. I and II

    C. I and III

    D. I, II, and III

    E. II and II

Answer: D

Explanation: The mode for the data set is 2 and 5 as these numbers appear the most. The number 2 appears in the textbooks sold and the number 2 appears twice in the study guides sold. The number 5 appears in all three study guides. Therefore, all three books contain the value of the mode.

QUESTION 31

Bill is ten years older than his sister. If Bill was twenty-five years of age in 1983, in what year was he born?

    A. 1948

    B. 1953

    C. 1958

    D. 1963

    E. 1968

Answer: C

Explanation: The first sentence of this problem is not needed as that is extra information. If Bill was 25 years old in 1983, subtract 25 from 1983 to obtain his birth year.

$$1983-25=1958$$

QUESTION 32

The following are the scores Todd made on his exams during the Spring Semester: 90, 90, 90, 77, 75, 100, 84, 82 and 71. The instructor drops the two lowest scores and replaces those scores with the two highest scores. What is the average of Todd's scores?

    A. 84.33

    B. 89.22

    C. 99.22

    D. 90.00

    E. 90.33

Answer: B

Explanation: The two lowest scores are 71 and 75, and the two highest scores are 100 and 90. The two lowest scores need to be replaced with the two highest scores. The following is the new score list:

$$90, 90, 90, 77, 90, 100, 84, 82 \text{ and } 100$$

To calculate the mean, add up all the scores to obtain the total value.

$$90 + 90 + 90 + 77 + 90 + 100 + 84 + 82 + 100 = 803$$

Divide the result obtained by the total number of scores, which is 9.

$$\frac{803}{9}=89.22$$

QUESTION 33

John had two grocery bags, and they were weighed to the nearest kilogram. The bags weighed 33 kg and 43 kg. If the combined weight was W kg, which is true?

    A. $76.5 \le W \le 77$

    B. $72 \le W \le 73$

    C. $74.5 \le W \le 75.5$

    D. $75.5 \le W \le 76.5$

    E. $76.5 \le W \le 77.5$

Answer: D

Explanation: The combined weight can be found by adding the individual bag weights, which would be 43 + 33 = 76. From the choices provided, the only valid statement is D because the number 76 falls in that interval.

QUESTION 34

The width of Marty's backyard is 43.2 feet and the length is 32.1 feet. What is the area of the rectangular shaped backyard?

    A. 150.5 feet^2

    B. 160.6 feet^2

    C. 150.6 feet^2

    D. 1386.72 feet^2

    E. 1368.72 feet^2

Answer: D

Explanation: To obtain the area of a rectangle, multiply the length by the width.

$$43.2 \times 32.1 = 1386.72$$

NOTE: Use a calculator for computation.

QUESTION 35

Circle <u>all</u> such answers.

Of the following, which is/are greater than 1.25?

125%   3/2   150%   2/3   12.5%

Answer: 3/2 and 150%

Explanation: Convert all options to decimals format.

- 125% = 1.25
- 3/2 = 1.5
- 150% = 1.5
- 2/3 = 0.6667
- 12.5% = 0.125

3/2 and 150% are the only two greater than 1.25. The question states only greater than and not greater than or equal to, so 125% is not an answer.

QUESTION 36

If x is a real number and an integer and completes the solution $x^4 = 16$, which statement is true?

A. x is less than 4
B. x is greater than 4
C. x is less than 2
D. x = 2
E. x=4

Answer: D

Explanation: Perform the following operation:

$$2^4 = 2 \times 2 \times 2 \times 2 = 16$$

QUESTION 37

Sports Day Teams

Number of Teams	Students Per Team
4	3
2	8
6	2

From the chart, how many total students are there?

    A. 12

    B. 13

    C. 40

    D. 44

    E. 23

Answer: C

Explanation: To obtain the total number of students, multiply the number of teams by the number of students.

$$4\times3 = 12$$
$$2\times8 = 16$$
$$6\times2 = 12$$

Total number of students can be determined by adding the above results.

$$12+16+12 = 40$$

QUESTION 38

If the area of a triangle is $A = \frac{1}{2}\times b\times h$, then what would be the area of two triangles of the same size and shape?

    A. $2\times h$

    B. $b\times h$

    C. $2\times b\times h$

    D. $b^2 h^2$

    E. A and B

Answer: B

Explanation: If the area of one triangle is $A = (\frac{1}{2})\times b\times h$, then the area of two triangles can be found by multiplying by 2.

$$2 \times \left(\frac{1}{2}\right) \times b\times h = b\times h$$

QUESTION 39

The following expressions are given:

$$Q = 4x - 3x + 18$$
$$W = 2x + 4x$$
$$A = 4x + 2x + 1$$
$$B = \frac{3x + 2x + 19}{12}$$

Which of the following provides the largest value if the value of x is 1?

    A. Q

    B. W

    C. A

    D. B

    E. A and B

Answer: A

Explanation: To solve the problem, insert 1 for x in each equation and perform the basic arithmetic operations. Doing so shows that expression Q is the answer.

$$Q = 4(1) - 3(1) + 18 = 19$$
$$W = 2(1) + 4(1) = 6$$
$$A = 4(1) + 2(1) + 1 = 7$$
$$B = \frac{3(1) + 2(1) + 19}{12} = 2$$

QUESTION 40

Circle <u>all</u> correct answers.

If Q is a negative integer, select all that must result(s) in a positive integer?

$$-(Q)-1 \qquad Q^2 \qquad Q+1$$

Answer: Q^2

Explanation: The integers contain all negative and positive whole number and zero. That is, the set is given by $\{\ldots, -3, -2, -1, 0, 1, 2, 3, \ldots\}$. The only correct answer is Q^2, because the square of any negative integer is a positive integer.

If $Q = -1$, using -(Q)-1, then

$$-(Q)-1 = -(-1)-1 = 1-1 = 0$$

which is not a positive integer or a negative integer.

QUESTION 41

A circular pool is 300 yards in circumference. What is the radius of the pool?

    A. $130/\pi$
    B. $150/\pi$
    C. $175/\pi$
    D. $190/\pi$
    E. $300/\pi$

Answer: B

Explanation: The formula for circumference of a circle is

$$C = 2 \times \pi \times r$$

Insert the value 300 for C and solve for r. Remember to leave the answer in terms of π as the answer choices are given in terms of π.

$$300 = 2 \times \pi \times r$$
$$\frac{300}{2 \times \pi} = \frac{2 \times \pi \times r}{2 \times \pi}$$
$$r = \frac{150}{\pi}$$

QUESTION 42

How many square feet of carpeting are needed to cover the area pictured below?

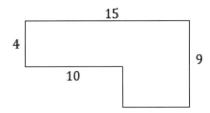

A. 45 square feet
B. 55 square feet
C. 65 square feet
D. 85 square feet
E. 87 square feet

Answer: D

Explanation: The figure provided is an irregular figure, so break it down into common geometric figures. Included in the figure are two rectangles separated by the dashed line. The area of a rectangle is the length multiplied by the width. To find the length of one of the unknown sides, use the given information.

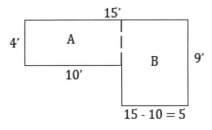

Area of rectangular A:

$$4' \times 10' = 40'$$

Area of rectangular B:

$$9' \times 5' = 45'$$

Total Area:

$$40' + 45' = 85'$$

66

QUESTION 43

Write the answer in the box below.

James walked 3 feet and 3 inches. The walk took 16 minutes and 15 seconds. What speed was James walking at?

in/second

Answer: 0.4 inches/second

Explanation: The key is to convert to the smallest unit. James walked 39 inches (3 times 12 plus 3). The time it took was 975 seconds (16 minutes times 60 seconds plus 15 seconds). Divide 39 inches by 975 seconds, resulting in 0.4 inches/second.

QUESTION 44

The table below shows the number of students who passed the math test with an "A" during a 5 month period:

Month	Number of Students
January	4
February	2
March	4
April	3
May	3

What is/are all the mode(s) from the data provided?

   A. 2
   B. 3
   C. 4
   D. 3 and 4
   E. 2 and 3

Answer: D

Explanation: Mode is the most occurring number in a set of data. In this data, there are two numbers that occur the most and the same number of times, which are 4 and 3.

QUESTION 45

If 3.49212×10^5 is expanded to an ordinary number, what number will be in the hundreds place?

    A. 4
    B. 9
    C. 2
    D. 3
    E. 1

Answer: C

Explanation: To convert the scientific notation to an ordinary number, move the decimal point 5 units to the right, since the exponent is positive, which gives the number 349,212. The hundreds place is 2.

QUESTION 46

What is $50\frac{1}{2}$ % expressed as a fraction in lowest terms?

    A. 101/2
    B. 100/2
    C. 51/100
    D. 50/2
    E. 2/1

Answer: A

Explanation: Convert $50\frac{1}{2}$ % into a fraction by multiplying 2 times 50 and then add 1, which gives 101. Then, convert it to a fraction with 101 in the numerator, and the denominator equal the denominator in the original fraction, which gives $\frac{101}{2}$.

QUESTION 47

In John's house, there are rooms for Joey and Victor. The length of Victor's room is 18 feet, and the length of Joey's room is twice as large. The width of Victor's room is 12 feet. What is the area of both rooms combined together?

    A. Cannot be solved.
    B. 216
    C. 432
    D. 423
    E. 261

Answer: A

Explanation: This problem cannot be solved as the question does not provide the width of Joey's room, which is needed to obtain the total area of the combined rooms.

QUESTION 48

If both a rectangle and a circle lie on a plane, determine the maximum number of intersection points?

    A. 2

    B. 3

    C. 4

    D. 6

    E. 8

Answer: E

Explanation: From the image below, the maximum number of intersections for a rectangle and a circle on the same plane is 8.

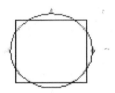

QUESTION 49

A distributor of clothing has three different types of packages. The first package can fit 10 shirts; the second package can fit 12 shirts; and the third package can fit 16 shirts. Large boxes using only one type of package will be made. If these boxes are required to have the same number of shirts, what is the smallest possible total number of shirts in one box?

    A. 180

    B. 220

    C. 240

    D. 260

    E. 280

Answer: C

Explanation: There are three different groups: 10 shirts, 12 shirts, and 16 shirts. To find the smallest possible total number of shirts in one box with only one package, it is necessary to find the least common multiple (LCM). The LCM is calculated by performing prime factorization of the three numbers in the packages. This is done as follows.

10	12	16	2
5	6	8	2
5	3	4	2
5	3	2	2
5	3	1	3
5	1	1	5
1	1	1	

The numbers were reduced to 1. The prime factors are those on the right of the chart above. Multiply the prime factors to find the LCM.

$$2\times2\times2\times2\times3\times5=240$$

The smallest total number of shirts in a box that is the same for all three packages is 240.

QUESTION 50

Write the answer in the box below.

8"

If the perimeter of the rectangle above is 64 inches, what is the width?

Answer: 24 inches

Explanation: The perimeter of a rectangle is 2l+2w. The length is given as 8", so solve for the width in the following equation.

$$2w+16"=64"$$

$$2w=48"$$

$$w=24"$$

QUESTION 51

Write the answer in the box below.

Six people plan to buy a computer for their coworker, sharing the cost equally. If one person decided not to participate, the cost per person for the other five people would go up by $16. What is the cost of the present?

```

```

Answer: $480

Explanation: The question requires setting up two equations

Equation 1 is $6x = y$, which is obtained from the statement: "Six people plan to buy a computer for their coworker, sharing the cost equally."

Equation 2 is $5(x + 16) = y$, which is obtained from the statement: "If one person decided not to participate, the cost per person for the other five people would go up by $16."

Variables: x = amount each student paid and y = total cost of computer.

The goal is to solve for y. The best way is to replace y in Equation 2 with $6x$.

$$5(x + 16) = y$$
$$5(x + 16) = 6x$$
$$5x + 80 = 6x$$
$$5x - 5x + 80 = 6x - 5x$$
$$x = 80$$

Insert x into Equation 1 to solve for y:

$$6x = y$$
$$6(80) = y$$
$$y = 480$$

QUESTION 52

Write the answer in the box below.

At an office, the manager earns 40% more than a first year employee. The employee earns what fraction of the manager's earnings?

Answer: 5/7

Explanation: Assume the employee makes $100. If the manager earns 40% more, he will earn $140. The fraction of what the employee earns with respect to the manager is:

$$\frac{\text{employee}}{\text{manager}} = \frac{100}{140} = \frac{5}{7}$$

QUESTION 53

Write the answer in the box below.

If, $2.5(z-8) = 4.5z - 18$, then $z + 2 =$

Answer: 1

Explanation: The first step is to solve for z:

Step 1: Distribute 2.5

$$2.5(z-8) = 4.5z - 18$$
$$2.5z - 20 = 4.5z - 18$$

Step 2: Isolate the variable on one side and the numbers on the other side. Subtract 2.5z from both sides and add 18 to both sides.

$$2.5z - 2.5z - 20 + 18 = 4.5z - 2.5z - 18 + 18$$
$$-2 = 2z$$
$$z = -1$$

Step 3: Insert $z = -1$ into the expression $z + 2 = -1 + 2$, which gives the answer of 1.

QUESTION 54

Write the answer in the box below.

One pen costs $0.30 and one marker costs $0.25. At those prices, what is the total cost of 18 pens and 100 markers?

$$\boxed{}$$

Answer: $30.40

Explanation: Use the calculator to solve for the answer. There are two equations to solve, and add the results.

Equation 1: $18 ×0.30=$5.40

Equation 2: $100 ×0.25=$25

Add $25 and $5.40 which gives $30.40

QUESTION 55

Which of the following units is best for measuring the distance from Houston to Chicago?

    A. millimeter
    B. kilometer
    C. meter
    D. centigram
    E. milligram

Answer: B

Explanation: D and E are related to weight, so those are eliminated. A is an extremely small unit. A meter is also a small unit when considering Houston and Chicago. Best answer is B.

QUESTION 56

Circle <u>all</u> such answers.

What are the positive integer factors of 12?

        1   2   3   4   6   8   12

Answer: 1,2,3,4,6, and 12

Explanation: The positive integer factors of 12 are: 1,2,3,4,6, and 12.

Practice Exam 2

This page is intentionally left blank.

Exam Answer Sheet Exam 2

Below is an optional answer sheet to use to document answers.

Question Number	Selected Answer	Question Number	Selected Answer
1		29	
2		30	
3		31	
4		32	
5		33	
6		34	
7		35	
8		36	
9		37	
10		38	
11		39	
12		40	
13		41	
14		42	
15		43	
16		44	
17		45	
18		46	
19		47	
20		48	
21		49	
22		50	
23		51	
24		52	
25		53	
26		54	
27		55	
28		56	

This page is intentionally left blank.

QUESTION 1

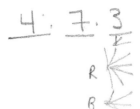

Which of the following symbols must be placed in the circle to form an accurate statement?

    A. =

    B. >

    C. <

    D. ≤

    E. A and C

Answer:

QUESTION 2

Kate has 4 shirts, 7 pants, and 3 hats. If each day she wears exactly 1 shirt, 1 pant, and 1 hat, what is the maximum number of days she can go without repeating a particular combination?

    A. 12

    B. 21

    C. 28

    D. 84

    E. 88

Answer:

QUESTION 3

In the number 3010, the value represented by the digit 1 is what fraction of the value represented by the digit 3.

    A. $\frac{1}{3000}$

    B. $\frac{1}{300}$

    C. $\frac{1}{30}$

    D. $\frac{1}{3}$

    E. $\frac{1}{10}$

Answer:

QUESTION 4

The normal price of a desk is $120 and the normal price of a printer is $30. An electronics store has a discount that offers a 30% discount on the printer when the desk is purchased at the regular price. What is the total cost of the desk and the printer at the discount price?

A. 150
B. 141
C. 129
D. 109
E. 66

Answer:

QUESTION 5

Which of the following is the best estimate of the value of the expression below?

$$\frac{(42,233)(491)}{9743}$$

A. 1000
B. 1500
C. 2000
D. 2500
E. 3000

Answer:

QUESTION 6

$$d = \frac{e^2 + f^2}{ef}$$

(e and f are positive numbers)

What is the corresponding change in the value of d if the values of e and f are each multiplied by 100?

A. It will be multiplied by 100.
B. It will be multiplied by 1000.
C. It will be divided by 100.
D. It will remain unchanged.
E. It will be multiplied by 50.

Answer:

QUESTION 7

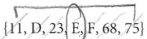

{11, D, 23, E, F, 68, 75}

If half of the range of the increasing series is equal to its median, what is the median of the series?

A. 22
B. 31
C. 32
D. 43
E. 64

Answer:

QUESTION 8

If Jake flips a coin twice, what is the probability that at least one head will be thrown?

    A. 0.25
    B. 0.45
    C. 0.50
    D. 0.75
    E. 0.85

Answer:

$$\frac{3}{4}$$

QUESTION 9

If $y = 15 \times 25 \times 32$, which of the following is NOT an integer?

    A. y/12
    B. y/15
    C. y/18
    D. y/20
    E. y/30

Answer:

$15 \cdot 25 \cdot 32$

$$\frac{3 \cdot 5 \cdot 5 \cdot 5 \cdot 8 \cdot 4}{3 \cdot 5}$$

82

QUESTION 10

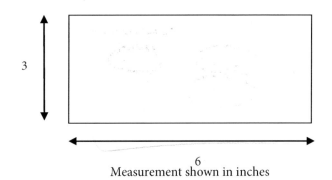

6
Measurement shown in inches

In the diagram above, the numbers are rounded to the nearest whole numbers. Which of the following is NOT a possible value of the area of the rectangle?

A. 8 square inches
B. 14 square inches
C. 19 square inches
D. 20 square inches
E. 22 square inches

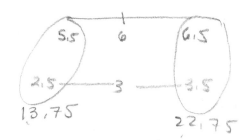

QUESTION 11

Each of the following is equivalent to 25% of 60 except:

A. $25 \times \frac{25}{100}$

$\frac{25}{100} \cdot 60$

B. 0.25×60

C. $\frac{1}{4} \times 60$

D. $\frac{60 \times 75}{300}$ $\frac{25}{100}$

E. $\frac{25}{100} \times 60$

Answer:

QUESTION 12

A line segment is defined by:

    A. 0 point

    B. 1 point

    (C. 2 points)

    D. 3 points

    E. 4 points

Answer:

QUESTION 13

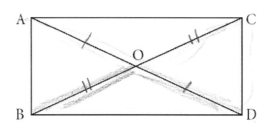

In the diagram, line CB and line DA intersect at O. If BC = -4x – 2 and OD = 2x + 5, what is the value of line AD?

    A. 2

    (B. 4)

    C. 6

    D. 8

    E. 12

Answer:

$$-4x - 2 = 2(2x + 5)$$
$$-4x - 2 = 4x + 10$$
$$-12 = 8x$$
$$-\frac{3}{2} = x$$

$$2\left(-\frac{3}{2}\right) + 5$$
$$2$$

84

QUESTION 14

In Barry's company, the ratio of the number of male employees to the number of female employees is exactly 2 to 3. Which of the following could be the total number of employees in the company?

    A. 88

    B. 96

    C. 100

    D. 112

    E. 124

Answer:

M M W w w

Parts

2

QUESTION 15

A machine can perform 40 identical tasks in 4 hours. At this rate, what is the minimum number of machines that should be assigned to complete 90 of the tasks within 2 hours?

    A. 4

    B. 5

    C. 7

    D. 8

    E. 9

Answer:

40   4

80

$\dfrac{40}{4} = \dfrac{10}{1}$

2hrs

10
10
10
10

20   20   20   20   20
1   2   3   4   5

QUESTION 16

A certain doctor earns n dollars for each individual she consults with, plus x dollars for every 15 minutes the doctor consults. If in a certain week she works 14 hours and supports 15 individuals, how much does she earn for that week, in dollars?

    A. 14n + 15

    B. 15n×15x+15

    C. $15n + \dfrac{14 \times 60}{15}x$

    D. $15x + \dfrac{14 \times 60}{15}n$

    E. $15n + \dfrac{14}{15}x$

Answer:

$15n + 14 \cdot 4x$

$14 \cdot \dfrac{60}{15}$

$\dfrac{60}{15}$

n = 10
x = 1

150 + 4.14

150 +

86

QUESTION 17

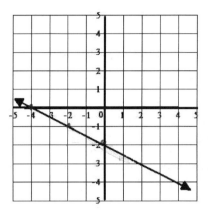

Which of the following equations represents the line above?

$y = (m)x + b$

A. $y = (2/4)x + 2$

B. $y = (1/2)x - 2$

$\dfrac{-1}{2}$

C. $y = -(2/4)x - 2$

D. $y = -(1/2)x + 2$

E. $y = -(1/2)x - 4$

Answer:

QUESTION 18

Two sisters decide to start a business. They will make and deliver balloons for special occasions. It will cost them $59.99 to buy the machine to fill the balloons with air. Based on their calculation, it will cost them $3.00 to buy the balloon and ribbon needed to make each balloon. Which of the following expressions could be used to model the total cost for producing b balloons?

A. $3.00b + $59.99

B. $54.99b

C. $3.00b - $59.99

D. $59.99b + $3.00b

E. $41.99b

Answer:

QUESTION 19

$$y = \frac{x+6}{x-6}$$

What are the domain and range for the relation above?

    A. Domain = {all real numbers}, Range = {all real numbers}

    B. Domain = {all real numbers ≠ 6}, Range = {all real numbers}

    C. Domain = {all real numbers ≠ −6}, Range = {all real numbers}

    D. Domain = {all real numbers}, Range = {all real numbers ≠ 6}

    E. None of the above

Answer:

QUESTION 20

The following steps are taken to solve the inequality:

Step 1: $3(x+6) \leq 5(x+2)$

Step 2: $3x+18 \leq 5x+2$

Step 3: $3x-5x \leq -18+2$

Step 4: $-2x \leq -16$

Step 5: $x \leq -8$

Step 6: $x \geq -8$

Which of the following step(s) did the student make a mistake?

    A. Step 2

    B. Step 3

    C. Step 6

    D. Step 2 and 5

    E. Step 3 and 6

Answer:

QUESTION 21

Jake has two rectangles, C and D, are similar. Rectangle C has a length of 100 inches and a width of 50 inches. The area of rectangle D is 200 square inches. What is its perimeter for rectangle D?

    A. 20 inches

    B. 40 inches

    C. 60 inches

    D. 80 inches

    E. 120 inches

Answer:

QUESTION 22

Given $f(x) = x^2 + x - 3$, find $f(-3)$,

    A. 3

    B. 6

    C. 9

    D. 15

    E. -15

Answer:

QUESTION 23

At Blake's Pizza, there are 4 types of cheeses, 5 meat options, and 4 veggie options. How many pizza combinations are possible?

    A. 13

    B. 16

    C. 60

    D. 80

    E. 100

Answer:

QUESTION 24

Use the table below to answer the question that follows.

Section	Total Number of Questions	Number of Questions Correctly Answered
Pre-Algebra	18	16
Algebra	12	11
Geometry	20	18

The above table shows the performance of a student on a math exam with three sections. What percent of the questions on the entire exam did the student answer incorrectly?

    A. 10%

    B. 30%

    C. 55%

    D. 75%

    E. 90%

Answer:

QUESTION 25

Mr. Martin needs to order rope for his afterschool physical education class of 24 students. The rope cost $1.50 per feet. Each student will get a piece of rope that is 4 feet 7 inches long. What is the total cost of rope Mr. Martin needs to order for his class?

    A. $36

    B. $90

    C. $110

    D. $165

    E. $1320

Answer:

MT
MW
MTh
MF

TW
TTh
TF

WTh
WF

ThF

QUESTION 26

A doctor works 2 days per week at a hospital that is open Monday through Friday. If the workdays are randomly assigned, what is the probability that the doctor will work on Monday and Wednesday?

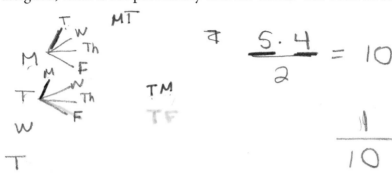

A. 2/10
B. 1/10
C. ½
D. 2/7
E. 1/7

Answer:

QUESTION 27

Use the diagram below to answer the question that follows.

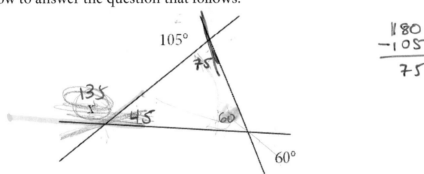

In the above diagram, the three straight lines intersect to form a triangle. What is the measure of angle x?

A. 135
B. 120
C. 75
D. 65
E. 45

Answer:

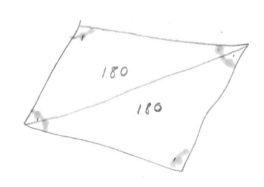

QUESTION 28

During a quality control check, a production facility found that 6% of the parts it produces are not aligned with the specification. The factory recently completed an order for 143,000 parts. What is the best estimate of how many of the parts from the order may be out of specification?

    A. 3,800

    B. 8,600

    C. 9,000

    D. 11,000

    E. None of the above

Answer:

QUESTION 29

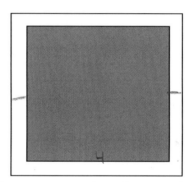

Two squares are shown above. The gray square length is 4 inches. The white square is 2 inches wider on each side. What is the perimeter of the white square?

    A. 8

    B. 16

    C. 24

    D. 36

    E. 48

Answer:

QUESTION 30

Jason uses 1 box of bird food every 5 days to feed the birds outside the church. Approximately, how many boxes of bird food does Jason use per month?

    A. 4

    B. 5

    C. 6

    D. 7

    E. 8

Answer:

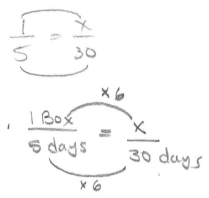

QUESTION 31

Mary has a bag of fruits. The bag contains 20 apples, 17 grape fruits, 12 bananas, and 8 peaches. Mary randomly takes one apple from the bag and gives it to her friend. What is the probability that she will next take an apple or a banana?

    A. 19/56

    B. 31/57

    C. 31/56

    D. 228/3136

    E. 12/56

Answer:

QUESTION 32

An elementary teacher has three packages of paper. One paper package contains 34 blue pages, another package contains 40 green pages, and the third package contains 70 white pages. If the teacher divides all the pages equally among 22 students, how many pages will each student receive?

    A. 5
    B. 6
    C. 7
    D. 8
    E. 9

Answer:

QUESTION 33

At the beginning of math class, half of the students go to the gym. One hour later, half of the remaining students go to the cafeteria. If there are 9 students remaining in the math class, how many students were originally in the class?

    A. 9
    B. 18
    C. 24
    D. 36
    E. 64

Answer:

36   18   9

start

$$\frac{1}{2}\left(\frac{1}{2}X\right) = 9$$

$$\frac{X}{4} = \frac{9}{1}$$

QUESTION 34

Jake got 12 questions incorrect on his physics exam and his score was 84%. How many questions were on the physics exam?

16

A. 60
B. 75
C. 80
D. 85
E. 90

Answer:

$$.16 \ X = 12$$
$$X = \frac{12}{.16}$$

QUESTION 35

The school policy is to have one bus driver and each bus cannot have more than 20 individuals (not included bus driver) total. The school policy is also to have two adults accompany every 15 students on school trips. With a total of 180 students, how many total seats will be needed for a school trip?

A. 192
B. 204
C. 214
D. 215
E. 220

Answer:

12   24
        180

        204

        11

QUESTION 36

What was the total number of games sold?

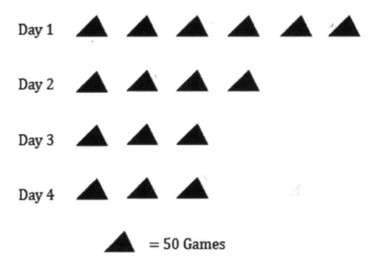

A. 600
B. 650
C. 700
D. 800
E. 850

Answer:

QUESTION 37

The following graph indicates the number of computers sold each week at a store. Estimate the number of computers sold in a monthly period. A month is approximated to be four weeks.

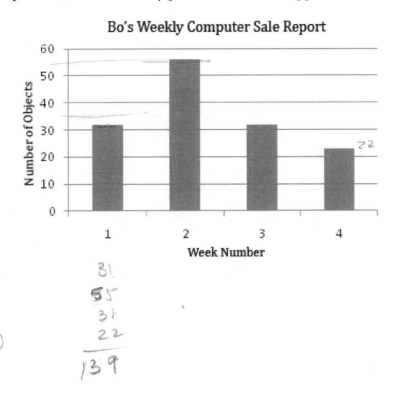

Bo's Weekly Computer Sale Report

A. 83
B. 97
C. 123
D. 143
E. 165

Answer:

31
55
31
22
_____
139

QUESTION 38

The following chart indicates the grade distribution in a college math class with 58 students. About how many students passed the class if at least a C grade is needed to accomplish this?

Percentage of Grades

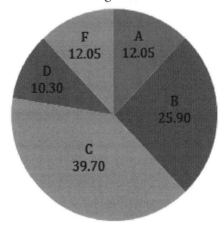

A. 48 students
B. 45 students
C. 42 students
D. 40 students
E. 39 students

Answer:

QUESTION 39

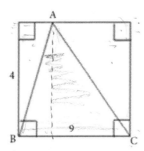

What is the area of the triangle shown above?

   A. 18

   B. 24

   C. 30

   D. 32

   E. 36

$\frac{1}{2} \cdot 9 \cdot 4$

Answer:

QUESTION 40

Which of the following equations does NOT represent a linear equation?

   A. $5x - y = 3$

   B. $-9x + 12y = -y + 4x$

   C. $y = 2x^2 + 4$

   D. $-\left(\frac{3y^3}{y^2}\right) + 6x = -4x + 5$

   E. None of the above

$x^1 \qquad y^1$

Answer:

99

QUESTION 41

Two kids are kicking a ball on the ground. If one of them kicks the ball at an average speed of 0.8 m/s and reaches the other kid 4 seconds later, what is the distance between them?

    A. 2.4 m
    B. 3.2 m
    C. 40.0 m
    D. 48.0 m
    E. 50.0 m

Answer:

$$\frac{m}{s} \cdot s$$

QUESTION 42

Which of the following is a common multiple of 16 and 60?

    A. 120
    B. 180
    C. 224
    D. 240
    E. 260

Answer:

2·2·2·2·3·5

QUESTION 43

The ratio of female to male teachers at a school is of 7 to 4. If there are 16 male teachers, how many female teachers are there in total?

   A. 21
   B. 28
   C. 32
   D. 35
   E. 37

Answer:

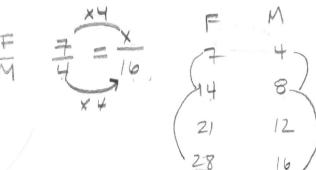

QUESTION 44

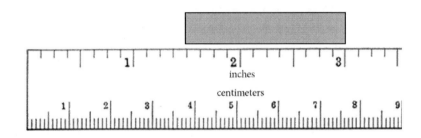

What is the best approximate length of the gray box?

   A. 3 inches
   B. 2.5 inches
   C. 2 inches
   D. 1.5 inches
   E. 3.5 inches

Answer:

QUESTION 45

James High School has 1000 students and 40% of the students failed the exit exam. If the data is represented on a circle chart, what is the angle representing the students who failed the exam?

A. 112
B. 144
C. 180
D. 360
E. 400

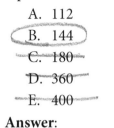

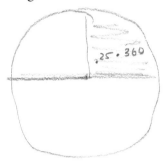

Answer:

QUESTION 46

17 18, 19, 20, 21, 23, 24, 26 27

Jake is asked to add two numbers to the above list. The requirement is that the median not change. Which of the following will change the median?

A. 17 and 27
B. 22 and 22
C. 21 and 21
D. 17 and 22
E. 18 and 23

Answer:

QUESTION 47

Which of the following is represented in above number line?

    A. -4<x<1

    B. -4<x≤1

    C. -4>x≥1

    D. -4≥x<1

    E. None of the above

$$\leq \times \leq$$

Answer:

QUESTION 48

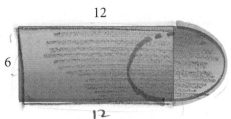

12

6

12

Which of the following expressions accurately reflects the perimeter of the figure?

    A. 26+3π

    B. 26+6π

    C. 30+3π

    D. 30+6π

    E. 32+6π

Answer:

$$\pi d$$

$$2\pi r$$

$$\frac{6\pi}{2}$$

QUESTION 49

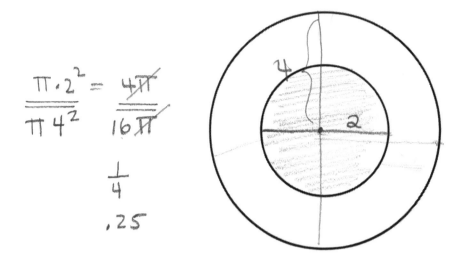

$$\frac{\pi \cdot 2^2}{\pi 4^2} = \frac{4\pi}{16\pi}$$

$$\frac{1}{4}$$

$$.25$$

The two concentric circles shown above represent a dartboard and they have diameters 4 and 8 inches, respectively. Given that a dart lands somewhere on the board, what is the probability of landing in the inner circle?

Write the answer in the box below.

$$\frac{1}{4} \qquad 0.25$$

Answer:

QUESTION 50

What is the scientific notation for the number 0.047?

Write the answer in the box below.

Answer:

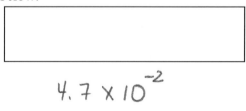

$$4.7 \times 10^{-2}$$

QUESTION 51
Circle all such answers.

$$-2x + 15 > 8$$

Which of the following values of x are solutions to the inequality above?

-1.65   0.75   3.89   3.21   3.70   3.14

Answer:

QUESTION 52
Circle all such answers.

$$\frac{1}{8}$$

Which of the following value(s) is/are equal to the above fraction?

0.125 $\frac{111}{888}$ 125%   1.25   12.5

Answer:

QUESTION 53

0.3 is 12% of what number?

Write the answer in the box below.

Answer:

QUESTION 54

Circle <u>all</u> such answers.

The weekly salaries of six employees at a local store are $40, $200, $140, $180, and $140. The value 140 is/are which of the following:

mean   mode   median   range   integer

Answer:

QUESTION 55

Use the graph below to answer the following question

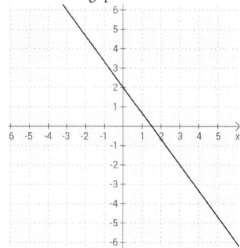

Which of the following equations corresponds to the graph shown above?

  A. y=2x+2
  B. y=3/4 x+4
  C. y=-4/3 x+2
  D. y=-3/4 x+2
  E. none of above

Answer:

QUESTION 56

The surface area of America is roughly 3.6×10^6 square miles. If a state has a surface area of 36,418 square miles, what is the best estimate for the ratio of the state's surface area with respect to that of the United States?

    A. 1 to 10

    B. 1 to 75

    C. 1 to 100

    D. 1 to 1000

    E. 1 to 10000

Answer:

This page is intentionally left blank.

Answer Key and Content Category Exam 2

Question Number	Correct Answer	Content Category	Question Number	Correct Answer	Content Category
1	C	II	29	C	III
2	D	IV	30	C	II
3	B	I	31	C	IV
4	B	II	32	B	II
5	C	I	33	D	I
6	D	I	34	B	I
7	C	IV	35	D	II
8	D	IV	36	D	IV
9	C	I	37	D	IV
10	B	III	38	B	IV
11	A	I	39	A	III
12	C	III	40	C	II
13	B	III	41	B	II
14	C	II	42	D	I
15	B	II	43	B	II
16	C	II	44	D	III
17	C	II	45	B	II
18	A	II	46	B	IV
19	B	II	47	B	II
20	D	I	48	C	III
21	C	III	49	¼ or 0.25	IV
22	A	II	50	4.7×10^{-2}	II
23	D	IV	51	-1.65; 0.75; 3.21;3.14	II
24	A	I	52	$\frac{111}{888}$ and 0.125	I
25	D	II	53	2.5	I
26	B	IV	54	mean, mode, median, integer	IV
27	A	IV	55	C	II
28	B	II	56	C	I

NOTE: Getting approximately 80% of the questions correct increases chances of obtaining passing score on the real exam. This varies from different states and university programs.

This page is intentionally left blank.

Full Math Practice Questions Explanations Exam 2

QUESTION 1

$$\frac{1}{4} \; O \; \frac{2}{3}$$

Which of the following symbols must be placed in the circle to form an accurate statement?

    A. $=$

    B. $>$

    C. $<$

    D. $\geq$

    E. A and C

Answer: C

Explanation: The best way to solve this problem is converting the fractions into decimals: 1/4 = 0.25 and 2/3 = 0.666. This clearly shows that the less than sign ($<$)is needed to make the statement accurate.

QUESTION 2

Kate has 4 shirts, 7 pants, and 3 hats. If each day she wears exactly 1 shirt, 1 pant, and 1 hat, what is the maximum number of days she can go without repeating a particular combination?

    A. 12

    B. 21

    C. 28

    D. 84

    E. 88

Answer: D

Explanation: Kate has 4 shirts, 7 pants, and 3 hats. To find the number of combination without repeating, multiply 4 shirts, 7 pants, and 3 hats to get 84.

QUESTION 3

In the number 3010, the value represented by the digit 1 is what fraction of the value represented by the digit 3.

A. $\dfrac{1}{3000}$

B. $\dfrac{1}{300}$

C. $\dfrac{1}{30}$

D. $\dfrac{1}{3}$

E. $\dfrac{1}{10}$

Answer: B

Explanation: This problem requires understanding the place value system and using fractions. To find the value represented by the digits, the place value system is used.

$$3010$$

$$(3 = \text{thousands}, 0 = \text{hundreds}, 1 = \text{tens}, 0 = \text{ones})$$

This represents that the number $3010 = (3 \times 1000) + (0 \times 100) + (1 \times 10) + (0 \times 1)$. The value for the digit 3 is 3000, and the value for the digit 1 is 10. Using fractions,

$$\frac{\text{value represented by the digit 1}}{\text{value represented by digit 3}} = \frac{10}{3000} = \frac{1}{300}$$

QUESTION 4

The normal price of a desk is $120 and the normal price of a printer is $30. An electronics store has a discount that offers a 30% discount on the printer when the desk is purchased at the normal price. What is the total cost of the desk and the printer at the discount price?

A. 150

B. 141

C. 129

D. 109

E. 66

Answer: B

Explanation: With the 30% discount, the printer will cost $9 less ($30 × 0.30 = $9). The printer will cost $21. Adding the $21 to the price of the desk gives total of $141.

QUESTION 5

Which of the following is the best estimate of the value of the expression below?

$$\frac{(42{,}233)(491)}{9743}$$

   A. 1000

   B. 1500

   C. 2000

   D. 2500

   E. 3000

Answer: C

Explanation: The best approach is to estimate the values given:

$$\frac{(40{,}000)(500)}{10000} = \frac{(4)(500)}{1} = 2000$$

Note: 4 zeros were removed from the top and bottom. Using a calculator is not recommended because it is a time consuming process.

QUESTION 6

$$d = \frac{e^2 + f^2}{ef}$$

(e and f are positive numbers)

What is the corresponding change in the value of d if the values of e and f are each multiplied by 100?

   A. It will be multiplied by 100.

   B. It will be multiplied by 1000.

   C. It will be divided by 100.

   D. It will remain unchanged.

   E. It will be multiplied by 50.

Answer: D

Explanation: Multiplying e and f by 100 has the same effect on the numerator and denominator. This allows for the effect to cancel, resulting in the same expression as originally given.

$$d = \frac{(100e)^2 + (100f)^2}{(100e)(100f)} = \frac{100^2[e^2 + f^2]}{(100)(100)[ef]} = \frac{e^2 + f^2}{ef}$$

QUESTION 7

$$\{11, D, 23, E, F, 68, 75\}$$

If half of the range of the increasing series is equal to its median, what is the median of the series?

    A. 22

    B. 31

    C. 32

    D. 43

    E. 64

Answer: C

Explanation: Don't get confused with all the variables. Range is the difference between the smallest term and largest term ($75 - 11 = 64$). The question states that the median is equal to half of the range, so the answer is 32.

QUESTION 8

If Jake flips a coin twice, what is the probability that at least one head will be thrown?

    A. 0.25

    B. 0.45

    C. 0.50

    D. 0.75

    E. 0.85

Answer: D

Explanation: The desired outcomes are HH, HT, or TH. Possible outcomes are HH, HT, TH, or TT. Of the 4 possible outcomes, 3 are desired, so the probability is $\frac{3}{4}=0.75$.

QUESTION 9

If y=15 × 25 × 32, which of the following is NOT an integer?

    A. y/12

    B. y/15

    C. y/18

    D. y/20

    E. y/30

Answer: C

Explanation: The first step is to solve for y, which is 12,000. The integer 12,000 ends with 0, so it is divisible by 15, 20, and 30 (based on divisibility rules). Answer choice A, y/12, results in an integer, which is seen by the fraction 12,000/12 = 1000. y/18 results in a non-integer (666.667), which is the answer.

QUESTION 10

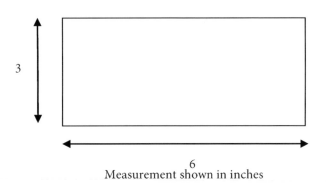

6
Measurement shown in inches

In the diagram above, the numbers are rounded to the nearest whole numbers. Which of the following is NOT a possible value of the area of the rectangle?

    A. 8 square inches

    B. 14 square inches

    C. 19 square inches

    D. 20 square inches

    E. 22 square inches

Answer: B

Explanation: As indicated in the question, the numbers are rounded to the nearest whole numbers. Based on rounding rules, the smallest possible values for the width is 2.5 inches. Anything under 2.5 inches will result in rounding down to 2. Based on rounding rules, the smallest possible values for the length is 5.5 inches. Anything under 5.5 inches will result in rounding down to 5. With the formula for area being length times width, the area is 5.5 times 2.5, which gives 13.75. The numbers can also be 3.49 and 6.49, which gives a total of 22.65. The values of the area are between 13.75 and 22.65. The answer is A.

QUESTION 11

Each of the following is equivalent to 25% of 60 except:

A. $25 \times \frac{25}{100}$

B. 0.25×60

C. $\frac{1}{4} \times 60$

D. $\frac{60 \times 75}{300}$

E. $\frac{25}{100} \times 60$

Answer: A

Explanation: 25% can be written as 0.25, $\frac{1}{4}$, and $\frac{25}{100}$, so B, C, and E are eliminated. In D, notice that 75/300 equals ¼, which be written as 25%.

QUESTION 12

A line segment is defined by:

A. 0 point

B. 1 point

C. 2 points

D. 3 points

E. 4 points

Answer: C

Explanation: A line segment will have one point at each end.

QUESTION 13

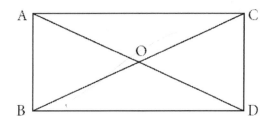

In the diagram, line CB and line DA intersect at O. If BC = -4x – 2 and OD = 2x + 5, what is the value of line AD?

    A. 2

    B. 4

    C. 6

    D. 8

    E. 12

Answer: B

Explanation: Line BC must equal line AD as the lines intersect at O.

$$BC = AD \text{ (Equation 1)}$$

The question only gives an equation for OD, so use the following relationship:

$$AD = 2 \times OD \text{ (Equation 2)}$$

Insert Equation 1 into Equation 2,

$$BC = 2 \times OD$$

$$BC = -4x - 2 \text{ and } OD = 2x + 5$$

$$-4x - 2 = 2 \times (2x + 5) \text{ (Equation 3)}$$

Solve for x in Equation 3,

$$-4x - 2 = 4x + 10$$

$$-8x = 12$$

$$x = -(3/2)$$

With Equation 2 and OD = 2x + 5, insert –(3/2) for x

$$AD = 2 (2x + 5)$$

$$AD = 4x + 10$$

$$AD = 4(-3/2) + 10$$

$$AD = -(12/2) + 10$$

$$AD = -6 + 10$$

$$AD = 4$$

QUESTION 14

In Barry's company, the ratio of the number of male employees to the number of female employees is exactly 2 to 3. Which of the following could be the total number of employees in the company?

    A. 88

    B. 96

    C. 100

    D. 112

    E. 124

Answer: C

Explanation: One approach to solving is to use the answer choices. With the ratio, "male employees to the number of female employees is exactly 2 to 3", the ratio for total male employees to total employees can be obtained as 2/5 (Note: 5 is obtained from adding 2 and 3). Using proportions,

$$\frac{2}{5} = \frac{x}{100} \quad \text{(x is the number of male employees)}$$

Solving for x,

$$2 \times 100 = 5x$$
$$200 = 5x$$
$$x = 40$$

With there being 40 male employees, there are 60 female employees, so establishing a fraction with male employees on the numerator and female employees on the denominator,

$$\frac{40}{60} = \frac{4}{6} = \frac{2}{3}$$

The ratio of the male employees to the number of female of 2/3 is obtained.

QUESTION 15

A machine can perform 40 identical tasks in 4 hours. At this rate, what is the minimum number of machines that should be assigned to complete 90 of the tasks within 2 hours?

    A. 4
    B. 5
    C. 7
    D. 8
    E. 9

Answer: B

Explanation: The key is to find out how many machines are needed to do a certain number of tasks in 2 hours. If one machine can do 40 tasks in 4 hours, in 2 hours it will complete 20 tasks. So, if there are two machines, that is 40 tasks, three is 60 tasks, four is 80 tasks, and five is 100 tasks. Using four machines is not an option, since the goal is to do 90 tasks.

QUESTION 16

A certain doctor earns n dollars for each individual she consults with plus x dollars for every 15 minutes the doctor consults. If in a certain week she works 14 hours and supports 15 individuals, how much does she earn for that week, in dollars?

    A. $14n + 15$
    B. $15n \times 15x + 15$
    C. $15n + \frac{14 \times 60}{15}x$
    D. $15x + \frac{14 \times 60}{15}n$
    E. $15n + \frac{14}{15}x$

Answer: C

Explanation: 15 individuals saw the doctor for which she will receive a total of 15n dollars. She worked 14 hours, which is equal to (14×60) minutes. For every 15 minutes, the doctor gets paid x dollars, so divide $(14 \times 60)/15$ and multiply by x to get the total amount of dollars the doctor received for working.

QUESTION 17

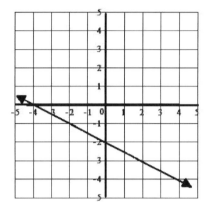

Which of the following equations represents the line above?

    A. y = (2/4)x + 2

    B. y = (1/2)x – 2

    C. y = -(2/4)x – 2

    D. y = -(1/2)x + 2

    E. y = -(1/2)x – 4

Answer: C

Explanation: Using the equation y = mx + b, with m being the slope and b being the y-intercept, y-intercept is shown on the graph as -2. The slope is -2/4 (go up two units and four units to the left; negative sign is due to going left). The equation is y = -(2/4)x – 2.

QUESTION 18

Two sisters decide to start a business. They will make and deliver balloons for special occasions. It will cost them $59.99 to buy the machine to fill the balloons with air. Based on their calculation, it will cost them $3.00 to buy the balloon and ribbon needed to make each balloon. Which of the following expressions could be used to model the total cost for producing b balloons?

    A. $3.00b + $59.99
    B. $54.99b
    C. $3.00b - $59.99
    D. $59.99b + $3.00b
    E. $41.99b

Answer: A

Explanation: The start-up cost is $59.99. The cost for each balloon is $3.00, so it will cost $3.00b to produce b balloons. Add 3.00b and $59.99 to get $3.00b + $59.99.

QUESTION 19

$$y = \frac{x+6}{x-6}$$

What are the domain and range for the relation above?

    A. Domain = {all real numbers}, Range = {all real numbers}
    B. Domain = {all real numbers ≠ 6}, Range = {all real numbers}
    C. Domain = {all real numbers ≠ −6}, Range = {all real numbers}
    D. Domain = {all real numbers}, Range = {all real numbers ≠ 6}
    E. None of the above

Answer: B

Explanation: Domain is all x values except x cannot equal 6 as the denominator will be 0. The answer is B. No restrictions exists for the range.

QUESTION 20

The following steps are taken to solve the inequality:

$$\text{Step 1: } 3(x+6) \leq 5(x+2)$$
$$\text{Step 2: } 3x+18 \leq 5x+2$$
$$\text{Step 3: } 3x-5x \leq -18+2$$
$$\text{Step 4: } -2x \leq -16$$
$$\text{Step 5: } x \leq -8$$
$$\text{Step 6: } x \geq -8$$

Which of the following step(s) did the student do incorrectly?

    A. Step 2

    B. Step 3

    C. Step 6

    D. Step 2 and 5

    E. Step 3 and 6

Answer: D

Explanation: In Step 2, the five needs to be distributed to the 2. Dividing a negative number by a negative results in the negative sign turning into a positive sign. In Step 5, it should be 8 instead of -8.

QUESTION 21

Jake has two rectangles, C and D, are similar. Rectangle C has a length of 100 inches and a width of 50 inches. The area of rectangle D is 200 square inches. What is its perimeter for rectangle D?

    A. 20 inches

    B. 40 inches

    C. 60 inches

    D. 80 inches

    E. 120 inches

Answer: C

Explanation: Rectangle C and D are similar, so the length and width of rectangle D must be proportional to the length and width of rectangle C. Moreover, the product of the width and length of rectangle D must equal 200 square inches. Taking the length of rectangle D as 20 inches and width as 10 inches gives an area of 200 square inches. The length and width also satisfy the condition that rectangle C and D are similar; multiplying 20 inches and 10 inches each by 5 results in 100 inches and 50 inches, which indicates similarity with Rectangle C. The perimeter of rectangle D is 20 + 10 + 20 + 10 = 60

QUESTION 22

Given $f(x)=x^2 + x - 3$, find $f(-3)$,

    A. 3

    B. 6

    C. 9

    D. 15

    E. -15

Answer: A

Explanation: Insert -3 in the function and solve,

$$f(x)=(-3)^2+(-3) - 3 = 9 - 3 - 3 = 3$$

QUESTION 23

At Blake's Pizza, there are 4 types of cheeses, 5 meat options, and 4 veggie options. How many pizza combinations are possible?

    A. 13

    B. 16

    C. 60

    D. 80

    E. 100

Answer: D

Explanation: Multiplying 4 types of cheese, 5 meat options, and 4 veggie options, gives an answer of 80.

QUESTION 24

Use the table below to answer the question that follows.

Section	Total Number of Questions	Number of Questions Correctly Answered
Pre-Algebra	18	16
Algebra	12	11
Geometry	20	18

The above table shows the performance of a student on a math exam with three sections. What percent of the questions on the entire exam did the student answer incorrectly?

    A. 10%

    B. 30%

    C. 55%

    D. 75%

    E. 90%

Answer: A

Explanation: From the table, obtain the total number of questions and total number of correctly answered questions.

- Total number of questions: $18 + 12 + 20 = 50$
- Total number of questions correctly answered: $16 + 11 + 18 = 45$

The question asks for the percent of questions the student answered incorrectly. To obtain that value, first subtract 45 from 50, giving 5 questions answered incorrectly. Then, divide 5 by 50 (total questions) and reduce the fraction by 5, giving:

$$\frac{5}{50} \div \frac{5}{5} = \frac{1}{10} = 0.10 = 10\%$$

QUESTION 25

Mr. Martin needs to order rope for his afterschool physical education class of 24 students. The rope cost $1.50 per feet. Each student will get a piece of rope that is 4 feet 7 inches long. What is the total cost of rope Mr. Martin needs to order for his class?

    A. $36

    B. $90

    C. $110

    D. $165

    E. $1320

Answer: D

Explanation: Convert 4 feet 7 inches to only inches:

$$(4 \times 12) + 7 = 55 \text{ inches}$$

Each student will need 55 inches of rope, and there are total 24 students, so the total length can be obtained by multiplying:

$$55 \times 24 = 1320 \text{ inches}$$

The question gives the cost per foot, so convert the 1320 inches to feet by:

$$\frac{1320}{12} = 110 \text{ feet}$$

The question states 1 foot cost $1.50, so the total cost of the rope is:

$$110 \times \$1.50 = \$165$$

QUESTION 26

A doctor works 2 days per week at a hospital that is open Monday through Friday. If the workdays are randomly assigned, what is the probability that the doctor will work on Monday and Wednesday?

    A. 2/10

    B. 1/10

    C. ½

    D. 2/7

    E. 1/7

Answer: B

Explanation: Total possible outcome is 5 (Monday, Tuesday, Wednesday, Thursday, and Friday). Probability of Monday and Wednesday being selected is 2/5. Let's say that Monday was selected, then the doctor has four days left and one possible outcome left (Wednesday), so probability is 1/4. Multiple 2/5 and 1/4,

$$\frac{2}{5} \times \frac{1}{4} = \frac{2}{20} \div \frac{2}{2} = \frac{1}{10}$$

In probability questions, if the word "and" is used, it likely is an indication to multiply.

QUESTION 27

Use the diagram below to answer the question that follows.

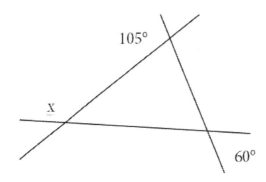

In the above diagram, the three straight lines intersect to form a triangle. What is the measure of angle x?

    A. 135
    B. 120
    C. 75
    D. 65
    E. 45

Answer: A

Explanation: The key is to find the angles associated with the triangle. The angle of straight line is 180 degrees. The angle opposite of intersection is equal to each other, such as 60 degrees and 75 degrees.

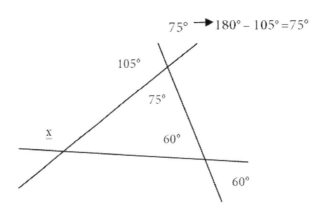

A triangle has 180 degrees. Knowing that one angle is 75 degrees and the other is 60 degrees, the third angle is 45 degrees (180 – 75 – 60 = 45). To find x, subtract 180 degrees from 45 degrees to obtain 135 degrees.

QUESTION 28

During a quality control check, a production facility found that 6% of the parts it produces are not aligned with the specification. The factory recently completed an order for 143,000 parts. What is the best estimate of how many of the parts from the order may be out of specification?

    A. 3,800

    B. 8,600

    C. 9,000

    D. 11,000

    E. None of the above

Answer: B

Explanation: Multiplying 0.06 by 143,000 gives the answer 8,560. The best answer is 8,600.

QUESTION 29

Two squares are shown above. The gray square length is 4 inches. The white square is 2 inches wider on each side. What is the perimeter of the white square?

    A. 8

    B. 16

    C. 24

    D. 36

    E. 48

Answer: C

Explanation: The gray square length is 4 inches, so all sides of the square are 4 inches. The white square is 2 inches wider, so the sides are 6 inches. To obtain the perimeter add 6 + 6 + 6 + 6 = 24 inches.

QUESTION 30

Jason uses 1 box of bird food every 5 days to feed the birds outside the church. Approximately, how many boxes of bird food does Jason use per month?

    A. 4
    B. 5
    C. 6
    D. 7
    E. 8

Answer: C

Explanation: The maximum number of days in a month is 31 days. Divide 31 by 6 to obtain 6.2. With 30 days in a month and dividing by 5, results in 6 as the answer. With 28 days in a month and dividing by 5, gives answer of 5.6. In each of these scenarios the approximate answer results in 6.

QUESTION 31

Mary has a bag of fruits. The bag contains 20 apples, 17 grape fruits, 12 bananas, and 8 peaches. Mary randomly takes one apple from the bag and gives it to her friend. What is the probability that she will next take an apple or a banana?

    A. 19/56
    B. 31/57
    C. 31/56
    D. 228/3136
    E. 12/56

Answer: C

Explanation: The total number of fruits is 20 + 17 + 12 + 8 = 57. If Mary takes one apple, the total number of fruits remaining is 56 with only 19 apples remaining. Then, the probability of selecting an apple is 19/56, and the probability of selecting a banana is 12/56. To answer the question of "the probability that she will next take an apple or a banana" add the two probabilities to get 31/56. The use of "or" implies adding probabilities.

QUESTION 32

An elementary teacher has three packages of paper. One paper package contains 34 blue pages, another package contains 40 green pages, and the third package contains 70 white pages. If the teacher divides all the pages equally among 22 students, how many pages will each student receive?

    A. 5
    B. 6
    C. 7
    D. 8
    E. 9

Answer: B

Explanation: The total number of pages is 144 (34 + 40 + 70 = 144). With there being 22 students, divide 144 by 22 to obtain approximately 6.55. The question states the pages are to be divided equally among the 22 students, so the total number of pages each student will receive is 6.

QUESTION 33

At the beginning of math class, half of the students go to the gym. One hour later, half of the remaining students go to the cafeteria. If there are 9 students remaining in the math class, how many students were originally in the class?

    A. 9
    B. 18
    C. 24
    D. 36
    E. 64

Answer: D

Explanation: Work this problem backwards. If 9 students remain in the math class at the end, there had to be 18 students before the students went to the cafeteria. If 18 students were in the class after half the students went to the gym, then the total number of students in the math class had to be 36 students. Now, work out the problem from the start. In summary, if 36 students were in the classroom, half of them went to the gym, so 18 students remained. Of those 18 students, half went to the cafeteria, so 9 students remained in the math class.

QUESTION 34

Jake got 12 questions incorrect on his physics exam and his score was 84%. How many questions were on the physics exam?

    A. 60

    B. 75

    C. 80

    D. 85

    E. 90

Answer: B

Explanation: Jake got 84% correct, which means he got 16% incorrect. The question to answer is "12 is 16% of what number?" So, $12 = 0.16x$. To solve for x, divide both sides by 0.16, which gives answer of 75.

QUESTION 35

The school policy is to have one bus driver and each bus cannot have more than 20 individuals (not including the bus drivers) total. The school policy is also to have two adults accompany every 15 students on school trips. With a total of 180 students, how many total seats will be needed for a school trip?

    A. 192

    B. 204

    C. 214

    D. 215

    E. 220

Answer: D

Explanation: The question is asking for total seats needed. To obtain the number of adults needed, divide 180 by 15, which gives the answer of 12, and then multiple by 2 (as two adults are needed for every 15 students). Total adults required are 24. With 24 adults and 180 students, the total number of individuals needing a seat on buses is 204. Each bus can hold 20 individuals, so to obtain the number of total buses required, divide 204 by 20 to get 10.2. The number of bus needed is 11 to hold all 204 individuals. In regards to seats, there will be 11 bus drivers, so the total number of seats for students, adults, and bus drivers is 215.

QUESTION 36

What was the total number of games sold?

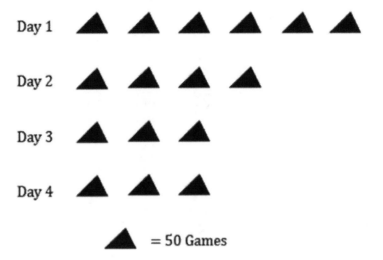

A. 600
B. 650
C. 700
D. 800
E. 850

Answer: D

Explanation: There are 16 triangles each representing 50 games; 16 times 50 = 800.

QUESTION 37

The following graph indicates the number of computers sold each week at a store. Estimate the number of computers sold in a monthly period. A month is approximated to be four weeks.

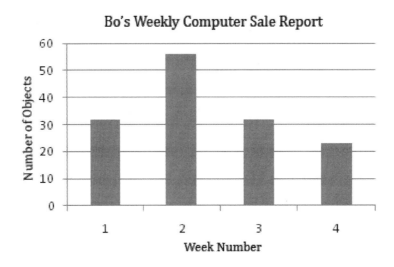

Bo's Weekly Computer Sale Report

A. 83
B. 97
C. 123
D. 143
E. 165

Answer: D

Explanation: From the problem, it is known that a month is approximated to be four weeks. Add the value of the bars indicating the quantity of computers sold.

number of computer sold=week1+week2+week3+week4
number of computers sold=32+56+32+23=143 computers sold in a month

QUESTION 38

The following chart indicates the grade distribution in a college math class with 58 students. About how many students passed the class if at least a C grade is needed to accomplish this?

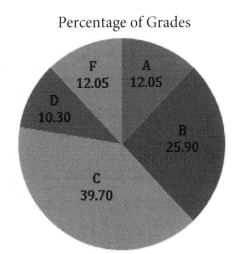

Percentage of Grades

A. 48 students
B. 45 students
C. 42 students
D. 40 students
E. 39 students

Answer: B

Explanation: The total number of students is given as 58. In addition, the percentage of students that passed the class can be calculated by adding the percentages for A, B, and C grades.

$$\text{percentage of passing grades} = 12.05\% + 25.90\% + 39.70\% = 77.65\%$$

Convert this number to a decimal form. To do this, the percentage needs to be 100, or simply move the decimal point two units to the left to obtain the same result.

$$77.65\% = 0.7765$$

Multiply the total number of students by the percentage written in decimal form.

$$\text{number of students who passed} = 58 \times 0.7765 = 45.037$$
$$\text{number of students who passed} = 45$$

QUESTION 39

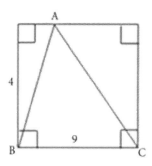

What is the area of the triangle shown above?

    A. 18

    B. 24

    C. 30

    D. 32

    E. 36

Answer: A

Explanation: The area of a triangle is $\frac{1}{2}$ × base × height. From the image, the base is 9 and height is 4. Using the formula, area is $\frac{1}{2}$ × base × height= $\frac{1}{2}$ × 4 × 9= $\frac{1}{2}$ × 36 =18.

QUESTION 40

Which of the following equations does NOT represent a linear equation?

    A. 5x-y=3

    B. -9x+12y= -y+4x

    C. $y=2x^2+4$

    D. $-\left(\frac{3y^3}{y^2}\right)+6x=$ -4x+5

    E. None of the above

Answer: C

Explanation: The question asks for an equation that is NOT a linear equation. Equations with the dependent variable having an exponent greater than 1 are not considered linear. A and B are eliminated. In choice D, the exponents can be reduced by canceling y^2 from the numerator and denominator of $\frac{3y^3}{y^2}$. Answer choice C is the only equation with the exponent of the dependent variable greater than 1.

QUESTION 41

Two kids are kicking a ball on the ground. If one of them kicks the ball at an average speed of 0.8 m/s and reaches the other kid 4 seconds later, what is the distance between them?

- A. 2.4 m
- B. 3.2 m
- C. 40.0 m
- D. 48.0 m
- E. 50.0 m

Answer: B

Explanation: The question requires using the formula: distance = rate × time. Multiplying 0.8 m/s by 4 s, gives answer of 3.2 m.

QUESTION 42

Which of the following is a common multiple of 16 and 60?

- A. 120
- B. 180
- C. 224
- D. 240
- E. 260

Answer: D

Explanation: The following are multiples of 16 and 60:

- Multiples of 16: 16, 32, 48, 64, 80, 96, 112, ..., 240
- Multiples of 60: 60, 120, 180, 240

Because 240 appears on both lists of multiples, 240 is a common multiple of 16 and 60.

QUESTION 43

The ratio of female to male teachers at a school is of 7 to 4. If there are 16 male teachers, how many female teachers are there in total?

    A. 21
    B. 28
    C. 32
    D. 35
    E. 37

Answer: B

Explanation: The ratio of females to males is 7 to 4. To solve for the number of female teachers, use proportion:

$$\frac{female}{male} = \frac{7}{4} = \frac{x}{16}$$
$$7 \times 16 = 4x$$
$$112 = 4x$$
$$x = 28$$

QUESTION 44

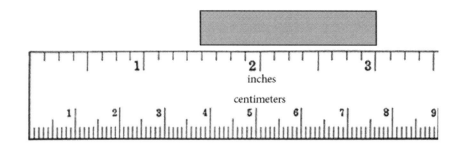

What is the best approximate length of the gray box?

    A. 3 inches
    B. 2.5 inches
    C. 2 inches
    D. 1.5 inches
    E. 3.5 inches

Answer: D

Explanation: Looking at the image, the length is approximately 1.5. The image starts at 1.5 inches and ends at 3 inches.

QUESTION 45

James High School has 1000 students and 40% of the students failed the exit exam. If the data is represented on a circle chart, what is the angle representing the students who failed the exam?

    A. 112

    B. 144

    C. 180

    D. 360

    E. 400

Answer: B

Explanation: Find the number of students who failed by multiplying 1000 by 0.40, which gives 400 students. The total possible angle value of a circle chart is 360 degrees. Giving the total number of students, students who failed, and total possible angle value of a circle chart, a proportion can get the value of the angle representing the students who failed the exam.

$$\frac{400}{1000} = \frac{x}{360}$$
$$400 \times 360 = 1000x$$
$$144000 = 1000x$$
$$x = 144$$

QUESTION 46

$$18, 19, 20, 21, 23, 24, 26$$

Jake is asked to add two numbers to the above list. The requirement is that the median not change. Which of the following will change the median?

    A. 17 and 27

    B. 22 and 22

    C. 21 and 21

    D. 17 and 22

    E. 18 and 23

Answer: B

Explanation: The median value is 21, and there are odd numbers in the list. To ensure the median does not change, find two values; one of which comes before the median value and the other that comes after. Only choice that does not satisfy the previous statement is choice B, which has two values that come after the median value.

QUESTION 47

Which of the following is represented in above number line?

    A. -4<x<1

    B. -4<x≤1

    C. -4>x≥1

    D. -4≥x<1

    E. None of the above

Answer: B

Explanation: The line is greater than -4 and it is also less than 1. Looking at it from the less than 1 perspective, the answer is not C. Also, there is a closed (solid) circle on number 1, so A and D are out. The answer is B because x is greater than -4 and x is less than 1 or equal to 1.

QUESTION 48

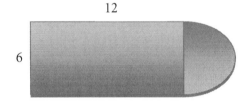

Which of the following expressions accurately reflects the perimeter of the figure?

    A. 26+3π

    B. 26+6π

    C. 30+3π

    D. 30+6π

    E. 32+6π

Answer: C

Explanation: There is a semi-circle, so the first step is to find the perimeter of the circle and divide by 2. Formula for perimeter of circle is:

$$p = 2 \times \pi \times r$$
$$p = 2 \times \pi \times 3$$
$$p = 6\pi$$

NOTE: The answer choices are in terms of π, so leave the answer in terms of π.

Divide the perimeter of the circle by half to get 3π. To obtain the perimeter of the rectangle, add only 12 + 6 + 12 = 30. The answer is 30+6π.

QUESTION 49

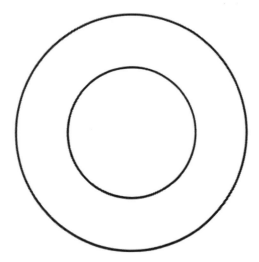

The two concentric circles shown above represent a dartboard and they have diameters 4 and 8 inches, respectively. Given that a dart lands somewhere on the board, what is the probability of landing in the inner circle?

Write the answer in the box below.

Answer: 1/4

Explanation: To find probability of landing in the inner circle, find the total area of the large circle and total area of the smaller circle.

Area of large circle with diameter of 8 inches:
$$A = \pi \times r^2$$
$$A = \pi \times 4^2$$
$$A = 16\pi$$

Area of smaller circle with diameter of 4 inches:
$$A = \pi \times r^2$$
$$A = \pi \times 2^2$$
$$A = 4\pi$$

To obtain the probability, divide the smaller circle area with the total area (large circle)
$$P = \frac{4\pi}{16\pi} = \frac{1}{4}$$

QUESTION 50

What is the scientific notation for the number 0.047?

Write the answer in the box below.

Answer: 4.7×10^{-2}

Explanation: Move the decimal point so that it is positioned between 4 and 7. The number reads as 4.7. The next and final step is to multiply by a power of 10 so that the value is 0.047. The power of 10 needed is -2 as the decimal point moved two places to the left when going from 4.7 to 0.047. The answer is 4.7×10^{-2}.

QUESTION 51

Circle <u>all</u> such answers.

$$-2x + 15 > 8$$

Which of the following values of x are solutions to the inequality above?

-1.65   0.75   3.89   3.21   3.70   3.14

Answer: -1.65, 0.75, 3.21, 3.14

Explanation:

The following steps are to solve the inequality:

Step 1: Subtract 15 both sides

$$-2x + 15 - 15 > 8 - 15$$
$$-2x > -7$$

Step 2: Divide both sides by -2. Multiplying and dividing by negative number requires flipping the inequality sign.

$$\frac{-2x}{-2} < \frac{-7}{-2}$$
$$x < 3.5$$

All choices less than 3.5 are the answers.

QUESTION 52

Circle all such answers.

$$\frac{1}{8}$$

Which of the following value(s) is/are equal to the above fraction?

0.125 $\frac{111}{888}$ 125%   1.25   12.5

Answer: $\frac{111}{888}$ and 0.125

Explanation: The key is to see if the options are equal to the fraction $\frac{1}{8}$. The fraction $\frac{1}{8}$ is equal to 0.125 in decimal form. Reducing the fraction $\frac{111}{888}$ results in $\frac{1}{8}$. The other options are not equal to $\frac{1}{8}$.

QUESTION 53

0.3 is 12% of what number?

Write the answer in the box below.

Answer: 2.5

Explanation: Convert the problem into an equation: $0.3 = 12\% \times z$

$$0.3 = 0.12 \times z$$
$$\frac{0.3}{0.12} = \frac{0.12 \times z}{0.12}$$
$$z = 2.5$$

QUESTION 54

Circle <u>all</u> such answers.

The weekly salaries of six employees at a local store are $40, $200, $140, $180, and $140. The value 140 is/are which of the following:

mean   mode   median   range   integer

Answer: mean, mode, medium, and integer

Explanation: To find the mean, add the values and divide by 5, which gives 140. The mode is clearly 140 based on the numbers provided. Arrange the numbers in order from least to greatest: 40, 140, 140, 180, 200, which shows that 140 is the median. The range is the largest number minus smallest number, which is 200 – 40 = 160. Mean, mode, median, and integer are the correct answers.

QUESTION 55

Use the graph below to answer the following question

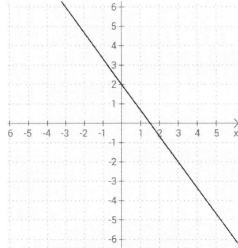

Which of the following equations corresponds to the graph shown above?

    A. y=2x+2

    B. y=3/4 x+4

    C. y=-4/3 x+2

    D. y=-3/4 x+2

    E. none of above

Answer: C

Explanation: Going down four units and three units to the right is the pattern shown in the graph, so the slope is -4/3. The y-intercept is 2. The equation is y=-4/3 x+2.

QUESTION 56

The surface area of America is roughly 3.6×10^6 square miles. If a state has a surface area of 36,418 square miles, what is the best estimate for the ratio of the state's surface area with respect to that of the United States?

    A. 1 to 10

    B. 1 to 75

    C. 1 to 100

    D. 1 to 1000

    E. 1 to 10000

Answer: C

Explanation: The first step is to convert the scientific notation into regular numbers by moving 6 decimal places to the right 3,600,000. The question states best estimate, so round the number 36,418 to 36,000. Divide the state's area with the United States area to obtain the ratio:

$$\frac{36,000}{3,600,000} = \frac{1}{100}$$

This page is intentionally left blank.

PRAXIS® CORE Math 5732

72284924R00086

Made in the USA
Lexington, KY
28 November 2017